A Compendium of Souls

The Dream Team of Spirit Helpers to Support You in Your Life

Angel Cusick

A Compendium of Souls

www.angelcusick.com
http://www.youtube.com/user/AngelBlog

ISBN: 1470080494
ISBN 13: 9781470080495

This book is dedicated to Grandma Cop and Aunt Dort. I miss sitting in your kitchen and drinking tea, and the money you wrapped in wax paper that was hidden in the cake. Thank you for giving me the best memories of my young life, teaching me how to grow cucumbers, and, most importantly, how to communicate with the animals. I will forever treasure those summers that seem so long ago, yet live so vibrantly in my mind. Thank you for all your gentle kindness and making me feel so loved. I hope you like the roses I sent to you in Heaven.

Disclaimer

Information provided by *A Compendium of Souls* is neither intended nor implied to be a substitute for professional medical advice or replace the services of a physician, nor does it constitute a counselor or therapist relationship. You should not use information in this book, or the information on Internet links from this book, to diagnose or treat a health problem; disease, mental, emotional, physical, or spiritual issue without consulting with a qualified healthcare provider. If you have or suspect you have an urgent medical problem, promptly contact a doctor. *A Compendium of Souls* advises you to always seek the advice of a physician or other qualified healthcare provider prior to starting any new treatment or with any questions you may have regarding a medical, mental, emotional or spiritual condition. Any application of the recommendations in these pages is at the reader's discretion.

"I love you when you bow
in your mosque, kneel in your
temple, pray in your church.
For you and I are sons of
one religion, and it is the spirit."

Khalil Gibran (January 6, 1883–April 10, 1931)
Gibran is the third best-selling poet of all time,
behind Shakespeare and Lao Tzu.

Table of Contents

Chapter Thirty

Isis

- Egyptian goddess with magical powers
- Ideal mother
- Goddess of children
- Patron of magic
- Love and sensuality
- Protector of the dead

Chapter Thirty One

Saint Francis of Assisi

- Talks to animals
- Helps you with any creature
- Writing

Chapter Thirty Two

Closing Thoughts

- Life in the spider's web
- Life synthetic in augmented reality
- A return to Eden

" *When I see ghosts they look perfectly real and solid—like a living human being. They are not misty; I can't see through them; they don't wear sheets or bloody mummy bandages. They don't have their heads tucked under their arms. They just look like ordinary people, in living color, and sometimes it is hard to tell who is a ghost.* **"**

— CHRIS WOODYARD,
Invisible Ink Interview

Introduction

The Scales of a Snake

I once met the man who built my grandfather clock, late at night in my 1880 carriage house in Chislehurst, Kent, England. The gentleman wore an immaculate three-piece suit with a watch chain dangling from his vest—time seemed to be of utmost importance to him. He had come back to ask—in horror—why I had wrapped a piece of "cotton" around the mechanical arm of his beloved "chronometer"? "What have ye done to me timepiece, lass?" A look of sheer panic twisted his kind features and he gasped for breath as he frantically asked the question.

I respectfully replied that the "Tampax" had been put there to keep the clock from chiming too loudly, often causing me to waken from deep sleep. He was a short, rotund and rosy-cheeked soul who blushed when I said the word "Tampax," figuring it was some kind of new-fangled fancy feminine protection. I guess none of this sounds odd—until I explain that the clock was built in 1732.

I told him I would take impeccable care of his creation and make sure only the best clockmakers around would be allowed to touch it. Upon hearing this, it was as though a thousand bells, whistles, and weights were taken off his little Hobbit shoulders. He then proudly told me it had once been the town clock at a shop in a small village in the north of England—but now he understood why I had "tinkered" with his work. Later on, when the clock needed maintenance, I hired only the best, knowing full well the clockmaker would be watching, holding his breath—not to mention me accountable.

I tell this story to elucidate the fact that there are all kinds of spirits, from all time zones, floating around and interfacing with us in ways that seem inconsequential. Here was a gentle soul who took such pride in his work, it extended so deeply into his psyche, that he needed to intervene if someone was compromising it some two hundred-fifty years later. I'm sure he smiled when he later saw an antique clock master—who wore white gloves and claimed he'd worked for the Queen—cleaning his humble creation.

The distinguished old English gent was equally appalled by my Tampax intervention as he "tsked tsked" me and shook his discriminating head. His disgust soon turned to delight though, when he discovered handwritten records tucked deep inside the clock's cabinetry. His eyes lit up through his sheer disgust, as he told me I had been the first person to clean the clock in over 111 years! I could literally feel the original time keeper jumping for joy, and the old but stately clock seemed to come back from some deep slumber, too. Commanded to remove the "lump of cotton," I sadly followed orders because, even with white silken gloves on, the clock master absolutely refused to touch it. Finally the clock could now chime in full glory. "Ding DONG!" the clock struck proudly, and I wondered if it, too, was ticked-off with my interference.

Back in the day, I attended The College of Psychic Studies in London, England, and that place kick-started what I already considered an intrusive, intermittent connection to something I had no interest in, under any circumstances, whatsoever. I had gone there specifically to make psychic thoughts go away, but, as time went on, I realized this wasn't something one could extricate perception from. With my analytical mind,

I was reluctant to partake of something I couldn't quantify or calculate. In the end, I learned the power in surrender and let the spirit world show me the path they insisted I stumble down, alone, with no roadmap to follow. I was a stranger in a strange land, but even worse, I was a stranger to my soul.

I grew up in a profoundly psychic family, with two grandmothers and even a great grandmother everyone regarded as "gifted." One of my grandmothers was the seventh child of a seventh child born with a Venetian veil. So, in the world I was born, third eye work was as generic as breathing; therefore, instead of questioning if it was there, I already knew it was, but just wanted it to cease and desist. The interference was distressing, especially since very few could understand the abstracted realm I was constantly propelled into. I wanted a normal life, but in the end I realized I'd have to follow the old adage that if you can't beat 'em, join 'em. So I did just that, dragging my knuckles, not wanting to take the leap that would turn me into someone I had no intent to be. I was a reluctant psychic, a reluctant medium, and a person unable to even admit to myself what I was, and the real world I was born into was a primitive place devoid of anyone or anything I barely had connection with, whatsoever. In other words, I was alone; even in a psychic family I was the odd man out. I often wondered, and still do, if I am even really human (on the inside)—and know many of you feel the same.

We are taught to be true to ourselves, and when someone tries to deceive their soul all manner of implosions occur, depression sets in, and a melancholy that strikes at the very core of your being descends. It's like an emotional prison that keeps you from knowing the truth, as reality distorts itself and one event after another lets you down. This occurs because when you are on the wrong path a succession of negative events unfolds, raising the stakes and making it harder and harder to follow that path, until you make a radical change— or suddenly give up on your dreams. When you follow the righteous path, all the universe accords and all manner of support you never imagined appears to make the path go swifter, sweeter, and easier to take. Finally, at the end of the trail, you have the added bonus of meeting kindred spirits and finding your proper place in the world. You become who your spirit wanted you to be. You arrive and finally have the ultimate reward: peace.

The media bombards us with images that insidiously force us to question our lives, marginalizing our accomplishments to something less than zero. We watch celebrities jumping on and off private jets, going to the best resorts, buying couture clothes, and delicately picking through rubble in their thousand dollar stilettos, as they show us how great they really are while half-dead third-world people greet their freshly exfoliated faces. There are some genuine ones, of course, like Angelina Jolie or Sean Penn, who really want to make a difference—but in general celebs stick to their glitz and glam, holed up in their mansions, and complain about their "leaked" sex tapes as they prepare to make another. It's a tough life, they moan, as they apply new hair extensions, and no one can even begin to understand the pain they are forced to fake.

The supersonic souls are those among us who are loving and kind and treat all life around them with respect. They are the unsung heroes who hold their families together, protect our country in the danger zones, rescue abused animals, and help that blind man cross the street. They are the meek, the humble, but mostly the kind, and their actions will bring them the brightest stars in Heaven. How they became so blessed is anyone's guess—but at the end of the day it's the energy of love they emit that will take them to the highest plane as their compassion sets them free. It is these people, of whom now I speak, that I want to impart this knowledge to and help you go even farther in the highest stratospheres of light.

Originally I had thought to create an anthology of particular spirits to call upon for support, direction, and intercession. I figured it would be most helpful to speak of souls I had actually met and who had imparted a wisdom that helped me in my own life. As I sat down to recall, a shudder ran through my veins—it was the first time I realized I had met so many. It was always very unexpected when they came- I wasn't looking for their particular help, and in fact didn't even know who many of them were, although like everyone else, I had seen their pictures or heard their names at some point in my life. I had no idea why they'd come to me, especially when they didn't seem like the kind of person I needed at the time. They weren't just saints and angels, but philosophers and musicians, film stars and scholars whom I knew little about— if anything at all.

I began to think of God as a giant snake with thousands of scales, and each one of those shiny armored pieces conducting special vibrations to help us on our way. God is at the head of the serpent and each scale represents one of his helpers, who graciously grants us the frequencies we require in our time of need. If you are reading this book, you were meant to know of these profound energy bundles you can call upon in times of trouble for yourself and others, including your pets. It's critical to ask for help—but what I'm repeatedly reminded by the spirit world is the importance of asking the right person the right thing. If you ask Grandma Cop for help with astrophysics, be prepared to get Grandma Cop's advice ("Oh, what a pretty green planet...").

There's a cornucopia of spirit helpers, waiting to assist on an almighty behalf, and all you have to do is put in the request. This tells us they will not violate free will, and in order to help us need our permission, not that they are politicians we need to beg or bribe. "*God helps those who help themselves,*" thus becomes a self-fulfilling prophecy as we take initiative to secure our future with a simple leap of faith by asking them for help. Most never realize how accessible these energetic spirals are, and therefore the endless possibilities to help propel you forward with your life.

Let's hope the little nugget in the middle isn't our prize but he probably is, considering Mayan timekeeping is less than one second off our modern day atomic clock.

A Righteous Neighbor

The world as we know it will no longer be what we once knew. Due to our coming new position in the dark galactic night, we spin in a direct convergence with the Milky Way galaxy, which will focus intense energy upon us, turning our planet into a highly magnetically charged place. Referred to as the Galactic Alignment, this configuration places us in a colossal energy field. The word Milky Way comes from ancient Latin and means "milky road." This interpretation was derived from ancient Greece, where it meant "milky circle," milk in ancient Greek meaning "galaxy." When we look up to the stars we see a little white wisp that seems to float gently in space. That romantic little bundle is, in fact, a galaxy that we can only see the sideways edge of. It spins over one hundred thousand light years away, containing anywhere from two hundred thousand to four hundred thousand stars, our solar system, fifty billion planets suitable for life, and one gargantuan black hole. It's considered to be as old as the Universe itself, and the new data coming out staggers the mind in its dimension and breadth. Whether we believe it or not, our alignment to it will impact our energetic life on physical, mental, emotional, and spiritual levels. How could it not? Look at what our little silver moon does to us women every thirty days! So this alignment arrives to induct us into our "new" age. It's an incredible moment to be alive, whatever you believe or even if you don't believe in anything at all.

The Age of the Jaguar

The Maya and other ancient civilizations foretold that man was now in his fifth attempt at survival, as we come to the very end of the last cycle on December 21, 2012, which has lasted, when added to the other four cycles, some twenty-six thousand years. On winter solstice, December 21, 2012, we are in a direct alignment with the Milky Way and that alignment ancient Maya called the "Dark Rift."

The Maya divided each of these ages into five categories with names according to how that age ended. The last cycle ended in 3114 BC, and they called it *the age of water.* Science indicates the entire earth at that precise last cycle was indeed historically flooded. The Maya called the age we live in now the age of the jaguar. Why? Because when a jaguar dies, it shivers and shakes. This indicates our cycle will end with major earthquakes and possibly, massive volcanic activity. Lucky us.

Suddenly standing at the brink of this energetic wave, our minds now have a supersonic ability to access vibrations that not only bring things magnetically to us, but shatter the glass roof of our three dimensional reality. We can access miracles, medical breakthroughs, and even other-worldly helpers, allowing us to exist in our wayward physical plane on a whole new vibration. In other words, we can now access a world we thought only existed in fairytales, a place that now shall, for the rest of time as we know it, collide intensely with our own. This is not a bad thing; one could even consider it a sort of deliverance—but one from our very selves.

Trending Stats for a Cosmic Generation

We've arrived at a critical conjunction where it becomes imperative that we ask ourselves what we want. What will make us happy? People asked this question over the millennia and all philosophers and scholars came up with the same thing: giving back to those around you—even if it's just a prayer, a kind word, or a blessing. Why, you ask? Because emitting a positive vibration boomerangs back to help you, the more we emit a good energy, the more we attract it. The way our chakras spin in opposing rotations turns our electromagnetic field into a magnet activated by our intent. Sir Isaac Newton, the father of modern day physics who's considered by some to be even smarter than Einstein, called our energetic constitution a "fluid magnet" that was activated by our intent. Today we call it an "aura" that can be photographed and documented by a special contraption that was initially inspired by the US military. It was originally called Kirlian photography, but now has become much more specific and sophisticated. The reason it's good to know you have this inbuilt mechanism called "chakras" (an ancient Sanskrit word meaning "wheels of light"; they can pull in or push out energy depending upon your intent), is because it's about to become a formidable tool for you in ways unavailable before at any point in human history. The Galactic Alignment will enhance your internal magnet, *so your thoughts are of primary importance at this time.* Negative mentalities now need to duck and dive at what comes their way, since we are about to enter into a potent magnetic field that responds faster, more intensely, and more acutely to our thoughts. It is of utmost importance that you stop, sit, and think about what it is you want to do for yourself and those around you. Who, exactly, are you?

Our nation is being dumbed down. Look at what we see on television and the Internet. We have gotten so far away from that driving force we once had, there are a multitude of distractions that pull us away from our focus. The Buddhists have a term for people that live over-scheduled lives causing them to not have the time to self-reflect, and that term is called "active laziness." You're busy, but too lazy to get the real job done of knowing who you are by not having the time to look at the self. A wise Chinese woman once said to me, "Why, with kids, you Americans care more about emotion... you forget about the mind!" At the time I didn't realize what she was saying was so true: people overindulge their kids to the point of making them helpless in the real world. The kids then assume everyone will think they're baby Jesus and become depressed when they realize people don't. The other problem from parents spoiling their kids is they accidentally erase their kids' threshold for pleasure, and once that dissolves, nothing makes them happy. It is here we enter into murky waters.

In the US they are bracing for the new generation becoming so disillusioned with life that there will be multitudes killing themselves, and by the year 2020, suicide will be the number two cause of death in the country (heart disease maintains the crown at number one). Now the fastest growing markets for anti-depressants are for preschoolers—not a good sign for the future. Why is this happening?

The new species born upon the planet are an evolutionary leap of consciousness and their heightened sensitivity to everything they see, hear, smell, and feel puts them at a heightened risk. Their sensory pads have not yet learned how to protect themselves, so everything we emit, our over-scheduled and complicated lives, or things they "feel" on the news, TV, Internet, etc. overwhelms their fragile auric receptors. They have incredible antennae about our interconnectedness with the living world but since previous generations became disconnected from it, the newcomers feel forced to live in an alien place. In the grocery store I have seen children in diapers horrified that their parents put meat into the cart, screaming that they "will never eat it!" as their befuddled moms look at them, wondering how on earth they got this way. The point being, they are highly evolved beings that are overly sensitive in a primitive world, and their defense mechanisms have not yet had time to grow protective shields. They are like walking little nerve cells on a cold and stomping planet.

So, basically we are looking at a species far beyond our development that can be equated to when Cro-Magnon and Neanderthals bumped into each other at the river. This is a generation that needs to be de-stimulated and stilled to study alone in their rooms and allow their shields to sprout—not shuffled around from pillar to post in a succession of mindless activities with no chance at neural recovery. In the Bible it says, "God created the world and on the seventh day he rested," which tells us energetically it's imperative to conserve one-seventh of our energy. I mention all of this because this is a precious generation of brilliant and powerful cosmic souls, and the last thing we want to see when we walk into their bedrooms is them swinging from a noose around their neck. I am sorry to be so harsh, but this is the cold, stark reality of what awaits us in the future. We need to prepare now. Today. This very second.

There is hope. Whether we understand it or not, we must teach the little sparks now, as well as ourselves, how to protect *energetically.* Tell them to imagine a gold bubble of light all around them. Have them click their fingers and see the gold bubble surrounding them and keeping them in a safe place. The ancient Chinese used silver swords, the Native Americans a golden gourd, the Egyptians used a golden goose egg. Tell them every time they click their fingers their bubble of light will come up. One simple click and their shields go up. This will not only keep their energy from being attacked by other people but, most importantly, keep them from hemorrhaging their light into the lesser evolved souls around them. They are ahead of practically everyone, and, according to the second law of thermodynamics, energy flows to a lesser source. Water, heat, everything finds its own level when set against itself. The children bear a greater risk because they are on a higher frequency, so everyone they come into contact with will energetically bleed them dry.

They also need one more critical component to their energetic constitution. They need to access earth energy, because it's something they innately block off, being cosmic spirits, but it's a necessary source in order to survive on this planet. The young, and most reading this book, will have an overflow of cosmic energy pouring in through the crown chakra at the top of the head. We must, however, maintain a symbiosis of earth and sky energy in order to function harmoniously within ourselves on the planet. Earth energy is important for things like money, love, opportunities, friends, the immune system—things that make life in this physical world pleasant. *It's your birthright, so you may want to use it.*

To access earth energy, first silently breathe a white light in through the top of your head and silently breathe out through the finger tips and toes. Breathe out any heartache, any sorrow, pain, grief, any negative energy you may well possess. Do this for a few moments until the pulsing ebbs away, then see golden roots growing out of the bottom of your feet and see them going down through the floor, down into the dirt, deep into the earth where there are crystals. Wrap your roots around these crystals. See the energy from those crystals gliding up through your roots as you breathe in through the bottom of your feet. You will feel a pulsing, a flutter, or a flow because this is where your foot chakras reside and they are the most potent of tools to feel better on the earth. This would be a great activity for you to do every night before going to sleep since it can easily be done in a bed while lying down. It's an effective technique to help anybody, young or old, support their energetic constitutions, which will help them get recovery in their sleep.

If you go to YouTube, I can lead you through accessing earth energy; just search:

How to Not Give Your Life Force Away and Avoid Energy Vampires.

Soul Food

In days of yore, there was a form of divination called "bibliomancy." This was a divinatory form begot from books—you ask a question and open the book to find your answer. You can use this book that way, or merely look into what particular worry you need to address and find the most appropriate spirit helper. Just know whatever you ask for comes with a level of responsibility, so be sure to ask for the right thing. You cannot bribe the spirits and swear to do something to make them help you, but you can give them offerings to thank them for their support.

Where applicable, there are also videos links listed from YouTube to witness first-hand the authenticity of the beings or situations recounted, so you can see with your own three eyes the reality of a situation. If you've never been on YouTube, simply Google it and you'll see a search button on top. If you join it, you can make comments and send videos to friends, but it's not necessary to join in order to watch videos. It's free and a phenomenal resource for everything under the sun.

I guarantee by the end of this book you will have a stronger faith, whatever you believe in, because this will bring it all home for you. I've also made some videos specifically for certain reinforcements in this book to help you get there faster. I recommend you use the links listed at the end of each chapter to deeply enhance the journey. It's also more profound if you *read the chapters slowly,* and allow the knowledge of each being to sink in, as you peruse YouTube links and see the profound, indisputable proof to support what is claimed. You are about to go on one of the most illuminating voyages of your inner life, so give yourself time to enjoy it sequentially, not gobbled down in a frenzy like french fries at McDonalds. Go slow and be in the moment—you will miss out on the energy infused if you don't give each chapter time to settle in to your unconscious, and you will only know these beings on a spindly, conscious state.

Speaking of food, in ancient cultures an offering of food was placed before the god or goddess for at least twenty minutes. The god would extricate the essence from that food and the beseecher would then eat the offering, which at that moment would be considered sacred food. Offerings can be anything from a bowl of peanuts to a candle, incense, a prayer, or even an orange. There are no limitations and in a sense when you bestow an offering to a God you inadvertently bless yourself.

So we stand at the crossroads of an oncoming vibration, perturbations propelled from our Milky Way in a direct alignment we haven't had to face in twenty-six thousand years, referred to as the "Dark Rift." This shift will shake the foundations of our beloved planet and cause the new generations to slip back to spirit, while at the other end of the totem pole, the older generations will not know what to do. In a sense the human race is being topped and tailed and no one down here really knows exactly what's going on. It becomes survival now to invoke support from the spirit world in whatever area concerns you and let them help you on your way. We are capable of creating miracles now, unlike any time before, and all we have to do is put in our request as we take a leap of faith. It doesn't matter what you believe or who you are in this mirage called life, because the spirit world responds unequivocally to cabbages as well as kings.

Let's get the party started.

"*The dreams which reveal the supernatural are promises and messages that God sends us directly: they are nothing but His angels, His ministering spirits, who usually appear to us when we are in a great predicament.*"

—PARACELSUS
*(1493 –1541) was a
German-Swiss Renaissance physician,
botanist, alchemist, astrologer, and
general occultist.*

"*Don't forget to send-up an offering.*"

Abundantia, the Minor Roman Goddess

CHAPTER 1

Abundantia

(You can call her "Bunny")

W e get the word "abundance" from this minor Roman goddess, who graced the ancient Roman coins for hundreds of years, starting in the third century. She was who you invoked for grain, gold, or even a baby, and on the coin she holds a horn of plenty that pours forth gold to all and sundry. Bunny helps us in the form of financial success, investments, ventures, business, and protecting that which we already have. Good luck, opportunities, and success are also under her protective care, and she likes to help us get through our fears over any sort of financial worry.

In Norse mythology she was called "Fulla," a girl Friday to Frigg who was the goddess of the clouds. She protected Frigg's most valuable assets, and often performed miracles for humans in financial distress on behalf of her beloved Frigg. According to the ancient Romans, *she brought these gifts of abundance while you slept,* and there was no limit to her level of giving—the more you ask her, the more she gives—but I can tell you first hand she likes to be thanked.

When I first met Abundantia, I found myself in a sumptuous hall with marble floors and golden sconces. There was a marble step up to a sort of raised dais where there were lots of golden silk pillows and red velvet drapes, and in the center of it all was a beautiful girl with dark hair, eating figs from a golden platter.

I assumed I was in ancient Egypt, as I watched this beautiful girl gorging on these figs in fast motion. All I could see was her profile, and as she ate the figs one after the other, I thought to myself "Oh, my god, I hope she doesn't choke eating so fast!"

At this moment the beautiful girl turned to look at me and laughed. "Ha ha! Oh, Angel, you're so funny!" It was at this moment I realized I must be out of my body since she heard me telepathically and also knew my name—as I instantly became aware of hers. It puzzled me that she was Abundantia, since I hadn't asked her for anything at that time. A young and beautiful girl, she was also nothing like what the masters painted. She had a very small turned up nose and was much younger than depicted.

She began to speak. "Angel, you teach your students about me, but you never talk of offerings or rituals. You know, the ancients sometimes gave me better offerings than what they even asked for." She looked at me with eyebrows raised as she chewed a fig.

I spoke using my lips. "I am so sorry! You are right. I never tell them to do that, but they need to know! I will make sure to tell them—I am so sorry Abundantia." I knew she was right and I thought of the rituals she said I never discussed.

She again telepathically answered. "Oh, rituals are just for you, to remind your mind to attract what it wants…what do you want, Angel?" She kindly gazed upon me as she popped another fig into her mouth.

I was overwhelmed at this point and stuttered, "Nnnothing! I'm okay, I don't need anything, but thank you!" I was honored just to meet this most radiant goddess.

She went on, using her lips to communicate. "Are you sure, Angel? There must be something…" A light hearted and playful soul, she really wanted to help me.

"No, thank you, but really…um…I am fine!" I said, wondering if I could take a rain check. She heard something that was barely a thought and answered back immediately with her telepathic voice, "Ask whenever Angel, that is fine! I am always there when you need me; just ask!"

At that point I slammed back into my body and could still feel her presence nearby. "Just ask." I could still hear her, ever so faintly, like a slowly fading dream. When I got up the next morning I went to the grocery store and bought a bag of figs. I put them in a small silver salt bowl in front of her picture (which doesn't do her justice). I bought a few of her coins from ancient Rome on auction at eBay and hold them If I speak to her in my meditations. Sometimes I wonder if the Romans knew what a sweet and playful girl she was, and how happy they must have been just to have her on their coins.

Invocation:

"Sweet Abundantia, eater of the figs, I ask thee to help me with all of my financial concerns. I would love to have more (your wish) to help me on my way, and know you are there to help me now and forever. Thank you, Abundantia, thank you for all your help—I am deeply grateful and thank you for spilling your cornucopia upon me in my dreams."

I made a video for you to watch about Abundantia on YouTube. Search for:

Attracting Abundance with a Roman Goddess and Sacred Offerings

The Golden Mean

"Anyone can become angry—that is easy. But to be angry with the right person, to the right degree, at the right time, for the right purpose, and in the right way—this is not so easy."

Aristotle (384 BC- 322 BC), *The Nicomachean Ethics*

CHAPTER 2

Aristotle

(Old Sandals and a Young Alexander the Great)

He turned out to be a most deeply pensive and thoughtful man. I had accidentally astral projected to ancient Greece when my encounter with him began, with a lot of activity going on in a field right behind him. Something large was being built—and it was definitely not a pyramid or a temple, because it was made of wood and it moved up and down. The activity was incredibly distracting, but I focused on the noble soul before me, who, like most, was as real as flesh and blood. I knew immediately I was in the presence of greatness, though I wasn't sure exactly who he was, and wondered if I should bow, genuflect, or curtsy as he kindly gazed upon me.

"My name is Aristotle," he said slowly and thoughtfully as he stood in a long white robe and worn out sandals. "You wanted to know about happiness, what makes the soul triumphant—is that correct?" I had indeed put out that thought but was not aware Aristotle was an expert on the subject—and honestly had no idea how I'd landed there before him. At that moment an angry young man came storming up to rudely interrupt us.

"Alexander, this is Angel. She has come to study happi—" as Aristotle introduced me, he sneered and turned his back on me and bellowed at Aristotle, "I need you to inspect this. Now." Aristotle reminded me of a battered wife who doesn't easily get offended by the abuser because she's so accustomed to it. Not batting an eye he replied, "I understand." Alexander stomped off.

Aristotle began to speak, but again we were interrupted—this time by a kindly, smiling man who handed him a pile of papyrus. I could see the oddest sketches of strange contraptions all over them. They looked like perfect, mathematical measurements of something large and awesome—maybe a machine used for digging or moving dirt. I didn't realize at the time it was a catapult. Aristotle looked at them and handed them back to the respectful man, saying, "It is accurate, my friend, yes." I didn't want to intrude or be disrespectful so I didn't ask a thing—though it seemed like it had something to do with Alexander and what was being built in that field.

Aristotle told me that the pursuit of knowledge was "the noblest of quests," and he wanted to teach me for my effort of coming through "the corridors of time" to see him. I remember wondering if it had been my spirit's intent to engage with this most erudite man, because on a conscious level I would never have thought to meet such a legend. He asked me if I realized the importance of finding out about who I was, and that it became more significant over time, because it impacted one's emotions throughout life. He said he thought the reason most people didn't make that discovery was because it would force them to live up to something they couldn't escape. He explained that most people were too lazy and complacent in their delusion of *who they weren't and what they could never be* as opposed to *who they really were.* He felt there was a repetitive cycle where people were given opportunities to discover themselves again and again, but most didn't wish to know why they were alive, and he considered this ignorance one of humanity's greatest atrocities. Aristotle's mind computed on a different scale, as he quickly moved from one profound concept to the next, in multiple layers in an interconnected way. He was about to tell me something else, when an angry Alexander interrupted us again, but this time full of rage and hostility directly aimed at me.

"Why do you persist in talking to this...this...*moron?*" He glared at me with venom and absolute disgust. It was obvious the man was a misogynist.

Aristotle raised his hand and replied, "What do you need now Alexander? I told Eudos the designs were perfectly accurate." Alexander spun into a hissy fit as he stormed away, reminding me of a diva used to hearing only yes.

I felt like I should leave, but Aristotle insisted I stay and not to worry "about the boy." He said Alexander was obsessed with warfare and was constructing a new weapon called a "catapult" to lob fire bombs at enemy camps. It wasn't until many years later I was to learn Alexander the Great was responsible for inducting warfare into a new age with his innovative use of catapults, battering rams and mobile towers, thus becoming King of the Macedonians by the ripe old age of twenty. It seemed, however, sweet old Aristotle was the power behind the throne who created the designs—but gladly let Alexander steal his thunder. Later I was to discover Aristotle had in fact been Alexander's mentor—even though when you put the two together they're like chalk and cheese (completely different). I often wondered what Alexander would have been like had he had a more tyrannical teacher, even though he was already out of control by age sixteen. Alexander's ego was so monumental that every city he later conquered he named

"Alexandria" in homage to himself—including the great city in Egypt that was later ruled by Cleopatra.

"I have spent many years unraveling the complexities of the human spirit," Aristotle calmly said, "and have in fact understood the reflection." I desperately tried to commit every word to memory as Aristotle continued his soliloquy.

"In order to find happiness one must first know themselves, who they are, what they are, and this takes deep contemplation. If you do not understand who you are, how will anybody else?" He looked deeply into my eyes, and I felt my soul puff up, perhaps happy to be educated. He went on, "One must be in a state of Eudemonia." I was lost by what he meant but knew he would explain.

"The second part of happiness is working on that part of yourself in order to make it better—become educated, study, travel, spend time expanding your knowledge. This takes time and dedication, but instills a formidable journey where one loses self to allow the soul to emerge. It came down here (the soul) to accomplish a task, otherwise one would not exist. If the soul is kept from accomplishing its work, a deep melancholy will pervade and overshadow the self."

"There is a third, most crucial, part, which is sharing the knowledge gained with the world. If it helps society move forward, even in the smallest way, a sense of joy shall flood one's life and create a force that will encourage others do the same. Sometimes the smallest contribution has the largest impact over time. Your action may inspire another who impacts the whole world, therefore you are part of an interwoven thread, ergo your small contribution becomes critical."

I wished I had a digital recorder for all the other things he said—and then he brought up his own teacher Plato (who was once a student to Socrates). "My good teacher inspired me with his analysis of joy. He believed in order to find happiness one must do three things. Be in a community, be needed in that community, and, finally, be loved by that community. I saw the relevance to his theory—but perfected it to a deeper understanding one could apply to their daily life." Aristotle let me process all his words, than quietly added another thought.

"Do you see how happy my apprentice Eudos is? I named my process after him because he provides a living example of knowing who he is, working on it, and emitting his light to the world. I do not pay him, for he is an apprentice and lives in great poverty—yet he is one of the happiest men I have ever known. We should all aspire to be like him."

I gazed down, accidentally looking at Aristotle's old sandals, barely held together that were worn, battered, and beaten. He chuckled, "One has no desire for material objects when the soul feels complete—and I feel bad for poor Eudos not even having sacks for shoes—but perhaps still it is time I need find some new ones…" He chuckled as Alexander interrupted us for the third time.

"Do you *not care* about me Aristotle? *Do you like to make me wait?* "Lightning bolts with thunder clouds seemed to blast out of his head, and I was really scared he would chop off one of my limbs, even though in a sense I was already dead.

Aristotle looked at him and calmly said, "You need show me respect, Alexander, as I show you. If you persist in demanding of my time I shall soon disrespect you, and if this is so you will have a weaker weapon. This I can promise." It was as though someone had poured a bucket of ice water atop Alexander, and he recoiled to scurry back to his alleged creation.

Aristotle looked at me, "Yes. I need new shoes. So easy to replace. Perhaps I will take Eudos with me and prepare him a set as well." He smiled as I looked at Alexander scowling at me from across the field. I knew it was time to go and dissolved slowly back into the physical world, wondering again if in fact it was Alexander the Great, Aristotle's greatest challenge, who inspired him to discover the Golden Mean—but what I pondered most was if Aristotle ever got those new shoes.

Invocation to Aristotle:

"Wise Aristotle, please show me the way to finding out who I am, as I promise to work upon myself and share it with the world. I wish to make society a better place in a large or small way, and I deeply thank you, Aristotle, for showing me the path to find myself and letting me help others on this voyage of discovery."

"Step into your grace. Sometimes you have to fight."

From the mind of Athena

CHAPTER 3

The Goddess Athena

(Girl with a Spear)

Known for her warrior strength, she was the ancient Greek goddess that Athens in Greece named itself after. The Parthenon sits on the Acropolis, a flat topped rock that rises nearly five hundred feet above the city of Athens. The Parthenon was the temple built to honor Athena while she guarded the city from her imperial seat. Ancient Greeks started building it in 447 BC and completed in 438 BC, though it was still being perfected with ornamental design until 432 BC (fifteen years under construction). A most revered goddess, Athena was to ancient humanity the ultimate deity invoked for wisdom, courage, inspiration, civilization, warfare, strength, strategy, arts and crafts, justice, and skill. She was the daughter of Zeus, and people often see an owl beside her because she inspires that image for people to focus on when they need her most. Often an owl will be seen as a portent to let you know she's protecting or providing you essential wisdom. Owls also are silent when they hunt; no one knows they're there until they've pounced. This dynamic can also be equated to the fact Athena's nearby, but you may never see her—only feel the impact she's graciously bestowed on your life.

I have never seen Athena, but our paths have crossed twice, and she performed one of the most jaw-dropping miracles of my life—but first I must tell you what happened decades before the main event, far away across the sea.

Back in the day, when I was young, I modeled in Europe, and in this season lived in a hotel right in the center square of Athens, Greece. The Parthenon was lit up at night and visible from the window of my hotel. I knew nothing of Athena, but was constantly drawn to look at the Parthenon and sensed a powerful strength I had never felt before in my life. I assumed it was because the temple was so ancient, magical, and magnificent that the vibration of all the people through the ages who prayed there imprinted its energy field, because it felt so good just to stare upon it.

My room had a single heavy gauge key, and I always put it near my bedside while I slept. On four different occasions, I awoke to the key bent into a spiral shape, making it impossible to use. When I brought it to the desk the first time the old man scratched his head—not speaking any English, he still gave me a perplexed look, then a new key. Over the next few weeks this happened two more times, and he started to think I had some sort of industrial device in my room that could spiral an indestructible key. The fourth time it happened, I made the mistake of saying he made "bad keys." His English-speaking worker heard and understood and graciously told him as all hell broke loose. They told me if I bent another key I was getting slung out through the fourth floor window. So I put that sneaky key in a sock in my drawer and luckily no more hocus pocus prevailed.

Now, nearly twenty years later, Athena came to my rescue—but once again got me in a strange predicament, making me wonder if "prankster" should be added to her list of attributes.

I have a school where I teach metaphysics and was working with my advanced circle teaching them about Athena. Nothing memorable happened; that is, until the very next day. The phone call came about eleven a.m. by the police to tell me my building was flooding from a defective fire sprinkler and I needed to get there ASAP. Heart in my mouth, I raced to the building and got there just as the fire trucks pulled up. I opened the door as gallons of water flooded my feet and my all-time worst nightmare began. The firemen wrapped my big furniture in giant tarps as the room rained like a torrential tropical storm.

There were legions of police, firemen, and damage control people standing in the five hundred square foot room as they drilled a hole in my ceiling to see how badly the water was trapped. I nearly hyperventilated but instead politely shrieked as they kept telling me not to worry, that the insurance would handle everything. Soon they had to go help the other victims in the building and everyone left my space while I stood in the pouring indoor rain facing the biggest disaster of my life. I was crushed at the amount of clean-up set before me, as I leaned on a mop, closed my eyes for a moment, and tried not to cry. Two seconds later I opened them up and saw, to my utter astonishment, *the entire room had not only stopped raining but was completely dry.* Everyone had left less than a minute before, and as I stood there leaning on my mop with my jaw wide open, unable to comprehend the sheer magnitude of the miracle, the damage control men came back because they forgot to ask me a question.

The two men dropped their clipboards and said, "My God, how did you clean this up so fast?" I was more shocked than they were, especially since the room had this beautiful golden glow and felt even better than before the flood. I didn't know what to say and replied, "Uh, I am good with a mop…" They said they'd never seen anyone clean a space so fast in thirty years; they looked at me like I was a freak but then excitedly asked, "Do you want a job? Would you consider coming to work for us?" I politely declined, as I reeled in a jubilee that the work was already done, feeling like Samantha in Bewitched.

About twenty minutes later a worker (who looked like Michael Jackson—could this day get any weirder?) came in with a strange long electronic stick as he silently poked it in various crevices throughout the laminate floor and various points around the room. I asked him what he was doing and he said he was looking for water damage from the flood. "This room is dry as a bone," he said,. "You're good to go." He turned to leave and I told him his stick must be broken and please to look at it again. Rolling his eyes, he told me to lick my finger, and after he pointed the stick at it an electronic beep went off. He walked out in a huff, telling me the room was completely dry. Not a moon dance to be found.

I knew I'd had the intervention of a higher force and knew it was Athena helping me since I taught her history the night before, and had asked her to help give me strength. In this epic flood I just didn't have the force to get the job done, and she used her warrior powers to help make it dry. I will always be grateful for her divine intervention, and it taught me an important lesson: *Ask for strength, because you never know when you may need it.*

Invocation to Athena:

"Great Warrior Goddess Athena, I ask you give me the strength to handle any situation (or name a pertinent situation) that comes my way now or later on in my life.

Thank you for granting me this power, Athena, and for blessing my life with your wisdom. Amen."

If you wish to see the Parthenon as well as the Agora and other ancient Greek structures, go to YouTube and search for:

Athens, Greece: Ancient Acropolis and Agora.
(I like this announcer because he sounds like an elf from a Christmas special).

The Acropolis in Athens, Greece

CHAPTER 4

What Is an Ancient Temple?

When we hear the word "temple," we think of it as a place to worship. Ancient temples were actually never used this way, but meant to serve as private abodes for the gods or goddesses who sustained that community. The needs of the gods were very important, especially since they controlled the forces of nature, such as the sun and rain that grew the community's crops, and the wind which drove their ships. Usually benevolent, the gods could turn against a community, so everyone wanted to please them. There were no atheists at this time. The gods had servants and received daily offerings of food and drink, including a proper share of the harvest, profits from trading and/or military conquests. Roman temples were festooned daily with plumes and incense.

The central part of the temple was occupied by a sitting or standing statue, once wood that eventually became stone, bronze, or gold. The statue of Zeus at Olympia, or Athena from the Parthenon in Athens, Greece, were made of "chryselephantine." Statues were built around an infrastructure of a wooden frame; thin carved slabs of ivory were attached to represent the skin. Sheets of gold leaf represented the garments, hair, armor, and other details of the icon. In many instances, glass and precious stones were also used for detail, such as eyes, jewelry, and weaponry. The statue of Zeus was considered one of the seven greatest wonders in the ancient world.

Only high priests were allowed inside the temple; outside there was usually a natural feature such as a spring, a cave, or a grove of trees, which were the actual focus for the public worship. If you were pregnant in the ancient days, you were absolutely forbidden from going into labor near these holy zones in the concern that, if you went into labor, you might sully the sacred grounds.

Religious festivals were dramatic events, and people wanted nothing more than to please the gods through wanton displays of devotion. The ancients were meticulous about paying their respects, since it was a widespread belief that if you neglect the Gods, the Gods will neglect you.

Go to YouTube and search for:

Ancient Temples to see temples from
around the world
or
Ancient Greek Temples (part 1),
which I particularly like.

"If you believed or disbelieved we could get through— but no one believes in anything anymore."

As spoken in a vision by my guardian angel

CHAPTER 5

The Angel and the Saint

The night I met my guardian angel and a cantankerous St. Pete

On January seventeenth, 2008, an abstract activity occurred when I left my body. I would have never expected this sort of event, since I was with a new boyfriend, and the last thing on my mind was God, angels, or any kind of saint.

I went on what seemed a long journey, finally landing before my guardian angel and a saint. They were sitting at a rickety old card table with empty cassette cases scattered all upon it. The empty plastic cases were white with no writing, except for one I could see quite clearly that had the word MAGDELENA written on the spine.

The guardian angel was a very rugged blond man with an incredibly kind disposition who had a brilliance that just seemed to radiate out into the room of light. At the time I could see his face clearly, but once the encounter was done his image was blotted from memory, and all I can recall now is a strong neck and a thick crop of shiny gold hair. He wore a white robe and was very relaxed as he sat on the left of a cranky hopped-up bony man in a brown robe, who introduced himself as St. Pete. St. Pete had a shock of brown messy hair, a small bony nose, high cheekbones, and a lot of disgust for those of us still trapped in the material world. I can still see his face, and he reminded me of a volcano always ready to explode. I was startled at this odd pair and had no idea what they had to say to me—especially at such an unholy time of day.

The angel spoke compassionately and said, "Angel (which was strange—he called me *his* name), you meditate every single day, but you never pray." I took in what he said and thought yes, that was correct, when, out of nowhere, St. Pete thumped the card table, making me jump about ten feet, and bellowed, "*The apathy!*"

I was trying to remember what that word meant, and as I stood there shaking, the angel calmly said, "He doesn't mean you, Angel—he speaks of the whole human race." He paused, then grimly stated, "If you believed, or even if you disbelieved, in God, we could get through—*but no one believes in anything anymore.*"

I was unaware of this growing trend and said, "But I do believe in God! I just thought it didn't matter if I prayed." The Angel shook his head sympathetically, and St. Pete sat ready to obliterate my essence. I continued. "I am so sorry. I will pray, I promise, every day. Can you please tell God that I'm sorry?" I was at a loss for words.

The angel said, "Angel, it's critical you have a dialogue with God." He paused, then added, "especially now." His words were poignant and spoke deep to my lethargic brain.

All of a suddenly we were whisked to a three-dimensional hologram reality. I listened intently as the angel pointed to the shape of a human being in the hologram. It showed a golden light entering in through the top of the head as the angel said, "This is what happens when you meditate." I watched divine energy pouring into the crown of the head, then the angel spoke again. "But when you pray, you need to also imagine a gold light pushing up and mushrooming out towards the heavens." I thanked him profusely for showing me this concept, and as I did, felt my soul collapse back into matter. I tried to recall what more was said but, like his face, much was expunged from my memory banks.

I looked up St. Pete and found he's the saint who controls the gates to Heaven. It made sense—the gates are within our own minds, and we just have to know how to reach them. Now I still meditate in the morning but pray every night, no matter what, every single day. As a sensitive person, you can feel the energy of God and his helpers in your life, and also their absence when you cease to invoke them. A hollow, depressing existence occurs for the soul when it's deprived of its realm, like putting a dog in the pound. He can take it for a little while, than he feels alone and full of sorrow but gets used to it. The soul doesn't like being kept in the human cage as it is, so at least let it have some connection to its realm, otherwise it can vacate the body and another soul can take its place—one who might not be so accommodating. How, you ask? By keeping the personality bound to terrible choices that lead it to a place of isolation, dissolution, struggle, and discontent. Why? To have the soul repudiate faith, therefore gaining control in a material world. Why would it do that? All dark forces want more souls in their battle against the light, and apathy makes you weak to their forces. This battle is called binary opposition or moral dualism, a fight that continually rages between the flesh and the soul. (First spoken about extensively by Plato [423-348 BC] in his dialogue Phaedo, Plato gives four arguments for why we as humans possess a transcendent soul at war with a physical body, that can be read about in his Theory of Forms.

Incredibly, some very disturbing facts just came out that indicate the angel was correct in his assertion that no one cared about anything anymore, because the "disconnected" are statistically on the upswing. This new emerging group is called the "Nones," meaning no religious identity, not even spiritually bound. They are also called "Apatheists," and both refer to a growing group of individuals who feel their destiny or life meaning has zero concern. Technology has become the new redeemer and Jesus is lost on the download. Instead of following any kind of religious or spiritual path, they would rather confer with their six hundred faceless friends on Facebook or Twitter. Seven out of ten young adults said they don't see the influence of God or religion in their lives at all. Here are the most recent statistics;

- 44 percent told the 2011 Baylor University Religion Survey they spend no time seeking "eternal wisdom," and 19 percent said "it's useless to search for meaning."

- 46 percent told a 2011 survey by Nashville-based evangelical research agency, LifeWay Research, that they never wonder whether they will go to heaven.

- 28 percent told LifeWay "it's not a major priority in my life to find my deeper purpose." And 18 percent scoffed that God has a purpose or plan for everyone.

- 6.3 percent of Americans turned up on Pew Forum's 2007 Religious Landscape Survey as totally secular—unconnected to God or a higher power or any religious identity and willing to say religion is not important in their lives.

It's like a cancer of the soul, the way people have inserted technology as their demigod instead of self-reflecting and making a connection to their own internal heavens. This connection to spirit requires a little time and effort, but people are so overloaded with stimuli now that this extra energy spent understanding it becomes too much wasted time; therefore, they become disconnected from themselves. This disconnect also gives the ego ample room to ramp up rationalizations that the entire meaning of life is random, and we are just like robots put here for no reason at all. If this disenfranchised generation looked any further, they would see that science itself equates our human design to being as random as a gale force wind slamming through an airport hangar and accidentally constructing a jumbo jet.

Moral of the Story: No matter who you are, you need to talk to God and ask for support. The happier you make your soul, the better life will be. If you ignore that huge inner portion of self you may overcompensate with your rational mind, but at the end of the day life will leave you hollow. *You are not a machine.*

Invocation:

> Dear guardian angel (or Spirit or God or whoever you believe), please let me hear my soul's wish for being here instead of Heaven. I respect its purpose and do all I can to honor its path now and forever.

*Atheists are probably snickering at what you may tell them. Let them, don't try to convert them. They will find out soon enough.

You can also go to YouTube and search for:

The Angel and the Saint

"Don't tell me their virtues, tell me how they overcame their weaknesses!"

Saint Bernadette (January 7, 1844-April 16, 1879)

CHAPTER 6

What Exactly Is a Saint?

S aints were created by the Catholic Church in the second century to distinguish exceptional people who impacted the faith with their exemplary behavior and indisputable holy powers. Saints care for every person of every religion and help achieve very precise results. They are not worshipped by Catholics, but invoked for support. Paintings and statues carry profound energy to help the seeker connect more closely to them. They are asked for intercession, akin to asking a good friend to ask God to do you a favor. They were people just like us, who grappled with issues from anger, drunkenness, public nudity, and even alcoholism.

The Catholic Church makes candidates go through rigorous, extensive, documented, and witnessed events in order to be proposed for the canonization of sainthood. Initial investigations are performed by the local bishop, who determines if this holy person lived a "venerable" life—meaning, did they lead a virtuous life, inspire with writings, perform miracles, die a martyr, or perform multiple miraculous intercessions from beyond the grave?

If their life legitimizes and validates the doctrines of the Church, the records are reviewed by a panel of theologians in Rome at the Vatican, where further evaluation ensues. This discriminating holy panel, called the Congregation for the Causes of Saints, determines whether the candidate should receive the rare and prestigious honor as a saint. If they approve the nomination, the pope proclaims the candidate "venerable." This is a monumental achievement that can still, at any point, for no reason at all, be cancelled or revoked.

The next step, beatification, requires evidence of miracles (except in the case of martyrs) from beyond the grave. This proves the being resides in Heaven and can help us when all else fails. This makes the candidate "blessed," and means they can be prayed to and honored by any group who holds them in high esteem. To recap the three stage process for becoming a saint is:

1. Person must be deemed "venerable"—meaning they exhibited heroic virtues in life.
2. Must have miracles attributed to them that are confirmed.
3. Must have other miracles attributed to their intercession after death—unless they are martyred for their faith.

Sainthood is a rare and holy event, because it provides indisputable proof that God works from Heaven directly through the saint. They will often appear in dreams when invoked and provide a deep sense of security upon interaction with them. They are the helper bees of God and have absolute compassion for the human race since they were once a part of the sacred code of life—unlike angels, who come from an otherworldly realm and are usually much harder to connect with.

One may note upon study of the saints' lives that many of them emerge from abnormally wealthy families. It can be imagined that God wanted people smothered and disgusted by money, who would go into a deeper state of devotion since worldly allures held no meaning for them. Upon further scrutiny, it seems one need go from one extreme to the other in order to fully embrace the whisperings of God, because his presence make an even more profound impact and his grace shines so wonderfully, that even a path of desire can't compete with what the Lord has to offer.

A really moving video on those blessed beings waiting to be canonized can be found on YouTube, and I suggest you watch at night to experience the incredible peace this touching video emits. Perhaps it's the actual photographs for many of these saints that makes them feel like old friends. **Search for:**

Faces of Modern Day Saints
for Atheists to Contemplate Video

What Exactly Is an "Incorrupt Saint"?

Not a requisite to become a saint, an incorrupt saint is often discovered by accident upon exhumation of their gravesite for a multitude of reasons. Incorruptibility occurs when God allows some humans (namely, saints), to stay intact and not decompose. A Google search will display incorrupt saints from all over the world and the shocking state of their mummification, or symbolic parts of their bodies with small or no decomposition even a thousand years later. Often their bodies also give off a fragrant scent that has been dubbed "the odor of sanctity." Often the entire body of the saint stays intact, and this phenomenon has yet to be understood by ongoing, rigorous scientific research.

All Saints Holy Day is on November first, so you may want to burn a candle to one or all. Whoever you are, please feel free to invoke them, whatever religion you follow (if any). They are people, celestial servants, and they want to help you in your life.

Go to YouTube and search for:

Incorrupt Bodies of the Saints
Don't be offended—not by the dead bodies, but the cheesy music!

"*Attribute to God every good that you have received. If you take credit for something that does not belong to you, you will be guilty of theft.*"

St. Anthony (August 15, 1195_June 13, 1231)

CHAPTER 7

Saint Anthony

St. Anthony is revered all over the world as the Patron Saint for lost articles, and is credited with many miracles involving lost people, lost things, and even lost spiritual directives. Saint Anthony is known in Portugal, Spain, and Brazil as the marriage saint, because there are so many legends of him reconciling couples. He also had the gift of oration—and his tongue, kept in a sacred reliquary, still hangs incorrupt.

Growing up wasn't always easy in the rock-n-roll town of Cleveland—even though I *love* the place. I was an incredibly ugly, rather hideous looking kid that was often mistaken for a boy even by nurses at the hospital. Being a scrawny, unpleasant looking child could make life difficult—people treat you differently when it looks like you've been hit by an ugly stick—but it was actually a good thing, because I was forced to think for myself and even developed something called a personality. I'm sure there are a lot of people reading this who know exactly what I mean. It actually infuriates me when people don't acknowledge it either, because it had a huge impact on my character, and the least they could do, after all the pain I endured, is to admit "Yes, you were repulsive."

After a while it got in my way. Being ugly wasn't fun, and it hurt that I was the girl who was the "friend" to all the boys who looked at me as one of them (the fact I kicked their butts in baseball didn't help my cause, either). After this cute boy on the telephone accidentally thought he was talking to my pretty friend and referred to me as "your ugly girlfriend," I realized it was time to fight back. Did I buy makeup? No. Did I get a new haircut? No. Did I get some new clothes? No. I had no money since I was only in eighth grade, so these options didn't even come to mind. Being a good little Catholic girl, I knew it was time to call in the big guns: I decided to do a novena to St. Anthony.

I chose St. Anthony because I figured if he could find things missing, he could help me find my face. A novena is praying to the same saint for the same concern for nine days in a row. You do not have to be Catholic to borrow the intercession of a saint, and we do not worship these benevolent souls; rather we *venerate* them and ask them to be our wingmen to God. They perform the miracle because they are graced to do so from a higher power—remember what I said before (in the introduction) about the scales of a snake? St. Anthony is one of those big scales probably near the head.

There are novena prayers you can find online for any saint and some of them will deeply move you. Prayers written from a thousand to even a century ago were written with such trust and innocence they make you drop all your defenses and allow the spirit near. I knew several novenas to St. Anthony and needed him the way some people need a drink. Getting to know his presence was truly a magnificent experience.

In the giant church of Our Lady of Angels, in the front upper right hand corner, was a giant statue of St. Anthony and before him in the dimly lit alcove was a collection of candles burning bright from other hopeful seekers praying he would grant their request. Once when I was sitting in the pew, a very old man came up to me and asked me if I were doing a novena to St. Anthony since he had seen me there before. I was startled, since people rarely spoke to others in church, especially a hot little mess like me. I answered "yes," and the old man told me this story about how St. Anthony answered his deepest prayer.

"Do you see this ring?" the old man held up a gnarled fist and I saw his wedding ring. "It was lost for fifty years. It was my wedding ring and it meant everything to me. I desperately wanted to find it, especially after the wife died." The old man shed a tear and wiped his eyes with a big white handkerchief. "I looked everywhere for decades, and couldn't find it. Fifty years passed, and I thought maybe it was high time to ask Saint Anthony to help me out." The old man gazed at the statue and a look of deep gratitude and love flowed out. "On the last day of the novena I went home. Something told me to go into the garage and look inside an old coffee can of nails in the garage. I looked inside." He paused and choked at this point. "There was my ring." I was about to respond, but the old man went on, this time lowering his voice. "Those nails were only about ten years old—there's absolutely no way I could have dropped my ring in there. I believe Saint Anthony *put* my ring in there—and showed me where to find it. So, trust in him. Whatever you need he will help you find it." The old man walked away and I was so excited I lit an extra candle.

Within days after finishing the novena I changed. Literally, totally and completely altered. Cleveland has the Rock-n-Roll

Hall of Fame, but the biggest rock star I ever knew was St. Anthony. It doesn't matter what you want, how small or big, you've just got to ask him to help you get it and have faith. When he died (at the ripe old age of thirty-six), because he actuated so many miracles, he was immediately granted sainthood by the pope. His legend, however, went on to scale even new heights.

St. Anthony was also a superb orator. When he spoke it commanded listening, and he was known far and wide for this additional gift of the tongue. Thirty-two years after he died, his body was exhumed, and though it was just dust and bones, his tongue was said to still "glisten in the sun." It was kept as a relic and is still, to this day, incorrupt. If you search online, you can see actual photographs of it, and it has been known that just gazing at the photograph can work miracles.

The 780-year-old relic was stolen in June, 2011, but distraught worshippers prayed and it was recovered three days later, so in a sense St. Anthony found himself with the aid of us. Glad we could help him out for a change. I know you must all be thinking what an idiot that thief was—like St. Anthony couldn't find his own tongue. She was caught and the tongue lashed out in its own way when the police pressed charges against her.

Moral of the Story: It doesn't matter what you're looking for, St. Anthony can help you find it.

Here is one of the many novenas to our beloved saint, in case you need something right away. Remember, all saints are equal opportunity miracle-workers; all they ask is that you have faith, but before you begin please first pick out a virtual candle.

Repetitive prayer said to St. Anthony for nine days before each Novena:

> O wonderful St. Anthony, glorious on account of the fame of your miracles, and through the condescension of Jesus in coming in the form of a little child to rest in your arms, obtain for me of His bounty the grace which I ardently desire from the depths of my heart. (*State your intention*)
>
> You who were so compassionate toward miserable sinners, regard not the unworthiness of those who pray to you, but the glory of God that it may once again be magnified by the granting of the particular request (*State your intention*) which I now ask for with persevering earnestness. Amen
>
> [Pray one "Our Father," one "Hail Mary," and Glory be to the Father, in honor of Saint Anthony]. Saint Anthony, pray for us!

DAY ONE

> O holy St. Anthony, gentlest of saints, your love for God and charity for his creatures made you worthy while on earth to possess miraculous powers. Miracles waited your word, which you were ever ready to speak for those in trouble or anxiety. Encouraged by this thought, I implore you to obtain for me the favor I seek in this novena (*State your intention*). The answer to my prayer may require a miracle; even so, you are the saint of miracles. O gentle and loving Saint Anthony, whose heart was ever full of human sympathy, whisper my

petition into the ears of the Infant Jesus, who loved to be folded in your arms, and the gratitude of my heart will always be yours.

[One "Our Father," one "Hail Mary," and "Glory be to the Father", in honor of Saint Anthony].

Saint Anthony, pray for us!

DAY TWO

O miracle-working St. Anthony, remember that it never has been heard that you left without help or relief anyone who in his need had recourse to you. Animated now with the most lively confidence, even with full conviction of not being refused, I fly for refuge to thee, O most favored friend of the Infant Jesus. O eloquent preacher of the divine mercy, despise not my supplications but, bringing them before the throne of God, strengthen them by your intercession and obtain for me the favor I seek in this novena (*State your intention*).

[One "Our Father," one "Hail Mary," and "Glory be to the Father", in honor of Saint Anthony].

Saint Anthony, pray for us!

DAY THREE

O purest St. Anthony, who through your angelic virtue was made worthy to be caressed by the Divine Child Jesus, to hold him in your arms and press him to your heart. I entreat you to cast a benevolent glance upon me. O glorious St. Anthony, born under the protection of Mary Immaculate, on the Feast of her Assumption into Heaven, and consecrated to her and now so powerful an intercessor in Heaven, I beseech you to obtain for me the favor I ask in this novena (*State your intention*). O great wonder-worker, intercede for me that God may grant my request.

[One "Our Father," one "Hail Mary," and "Glory be to the Father", in honor of Saint Anthony].

Saint Anthony, pray for us!

DAY FOUR

I salute and honor you, O powerful helper, St. Anthony. The Christian world confidently turns to you and experiences your tender compassion and powerful assistance in so many necessities and sufferings that I am encouraged in my need to seek you help in obtaining a favorable answer to my request for the favor I seek in this novena (*State your intention*). O holy St. Anthony, I beseech you, obtain for me the grace that I desire.

[One "Our Father," one "Hail Mary," and "Glory be to the Father", in honor of Saint Anthony].

Saint Anthony, pray for us!

DAY FIVE

I salute you, St. Anthony, lily of purity, ornament and glory of Christianity. I salute you, great Saint, cherub of wisdom and seraph of divine love. I rejoice at the favors our Lord has so liberally bestowed upon you. In humility and confidence I entreat you to help me, for I know that God has given you charity and pity, as well as power. I ask you by the love you did feel toward the Infant Jesus as you held him in your arms to tell Him now of the favor I seek through your intercession in this novena (*State your intention*).

[One "Our Father," one "Hail Mary," and "Glory Be to the Father", in honor of Saint Anthony].
Saint Anthony, pray for us!

DAY SIX

O glorious St. Anthony, chosen by God to preach his Word, you received from Him the gift of tongues and the power of working the most extraordinary miracles. O good St. Anthony, pray that I may fulfill the will of God in all things so that I may love Him, with you, for all eternity. O kind St. Anthony, I beseech you, obtain for me the grace that I desire, the favor I seek in this novena (*State your intention*). [One "Our Father," one "Hail Mary," and "Glory be to the Father", in honor of Saint Anthony].
Saint Anthony, pray for us!

DAY SEVEN

O renowned champion of the faith of Christ, most holy St. Anthony, glorious for your many miracles, obtain for me from the bounty of my Lord and God the grace which I ardently seek in this novena (*State your intention*). O holy St. Anthony, ever attentive to those who invoke you, grant me that aid of your powerful intercession.
[One "Our Father," one "Hail Mary," and "Glory be to the Father", in honor of Saint Anthony].
Saint Anthony, pray for us!

DAY EIGHT

O holy St. Anthony, you have shown yourself so powerful in your intercession, so tender and so compassionate towards those who honor you and invoke you in suffering and distress. I beseech you most humbly and earnestly to take me under your protection in my present necessities and to obtain for me the favor I desire (*State your intention*). Recommend my request to the merciful Queen of Heaven, that she may plead my cause with you before the throne of her Divine Son.

[One "Our Father," one "Hail Mary," and "Glory be to the Father", in honor of Saint Anthony].

Saint Anthony, pray for us!

DAY NINE

Saint Anthony, servant of Mary, glory of the Church, pray for our Holy Father, our bishops, our priests, our Religious Orders, that, through their pious zeal and apostolic labors, all may be united in faith and give greater glory to God. St. Anthony, helper of all who invoke you, pray for me and intercede for me before the throne of Almighty God that I be granted the favor I so earnestly seek in this novena (*State your intention*).

[One "Our Father," one "Hail Mary," and "Glory be to the Father", in honor of Saint Anthony].

Saint Anthony, pray for us!

May the divine assistance remain always with us.
Amen

May the souls of the faithful departed, through the mercy of God, rest in peace.
Amen.

O God, may the votive commemoration of blessed Anthony, your confessor, be a source of joy to your Church, that she may always be fortified with spiritual assistance, and deserve to enjoy eternal rewards. Through Christ our Lord.
Amen.

"Krito! We owe a cock to Asklepios! Don't forget!"

Socrates' last words

CHAPTER 8

Asclepios

A healer from ancient Greece who will come to you in dreams and remove your worst afflictions.

You are probably wondering who this wonder soul could possibly be, and if you asked this in the fifth century BC, you would probably be considered the village idiot. Asclepius (in ancient Greek, spelled Asklepios) even integrates into our life today, yet we sit oblivious to his legendary status, which still honored all around the world. The word "ask" comes from his name, because he was so popular in ancient civilizations that everyone requested his assistance. The word "therapist" comes from his attendants who were originally called "therapeutics," which in ancient Greek meant "attendant of the soul." His worldwide fame as the "barefoot healer" stretched from Asia Minor to Rome, and there were over 2,500 healing sanctuaries that people flocked to for over six hundred (some say two thousand) years before Christ. He was considered the consummate medical intercessor, and some of his temples are still used today.

Before Christianity, the ancients believed that prayer was not enough for healing—that one also had to access transpersonal dimensions where the soul was sustained and help dispensed for all portions of self, be it spiritual, emotional, mental, or physical. We have long since lost that connection, a psycho-spiritual energy resource that has more impact on our psyche than anything known. Even Dr. Dean Ornish, the eminent cardiologist, states that meditation is more important than diet or exercise. Nowadays, pain is drugged and denied, and spiritual epiphanies are disregarded. One must always remember that dreams are events that occur to the soul in an otherworldly dimension. In ancient days, the most educated people, of the highest intellect (i.e. mathematicians, astronomers, philosophers, etc.), all invoked Asclepius in order to get healing—and they would never waste their treasured time if the process didn't work.

Part of Asclepiad philosophy states we must immerse ourselves in nature, to re-enter the living web from which we came—and watch how it responds to us within it. Asclepiad dream healing did just that when the entire protocol was properly followed, and a significant part of this study was called the "dream incubation." In ancient days the process was strictly adhered to, and I shall now take you on the ancient journey exploring this miraculous healing. Museums have since emerged, because of the amount of recorded historical data accompanying this most remarkable healer.

The flagship temple for Asclepiad healing was called Epidaurus, about an hour and fifty minute drive from Athens, Greece. Before one even showed up, there was sacrosanct preparation done in order to receive the maximum amount of healing. Let's make an avatar and call our seeker Nikos.

At sunrise, Nikos would have spent the night somewhere near Epidaurus, so he could awaken, pray, meditate, and ask Apollo for forgiveness, because the ancients believed this was key for opening doors to the spirit world. If one held on to any negative thoughts, this would limit the seeker's ability to access the higher emanations of the Universe. So ask Spirit to help you forgive those who have hurt you, as well as those whom you have hurt, and ask spirit to help you forgive *yourself*. Forgiveness is a critical part of the healing process (please read this sentence fifty times, and then read it again).

Nikos would then fast, and perform an ablution—in this case a form of ceremonial cleansing of the body to remove the impurities of the flesh. Nikos would want to enter the ceremony clean and chaste, inside, outside and all around. He would want to show a reverence for the spirit world, and how you approached the ceremony deeply impaced your final results. If you disrespected the gods they could also do you harm, so reverence ran deep when you entered into sacred realms.

Nikos would only wear white to signify the purity of his intent.

Nikos would now make the journey to Epidaurus in a quiet state of mind, praying, fasting, and asking for more forgiveness.

Upon his arrival at Epidaurus, he would see crowds pressing to get into the giant iron gates that would only open at a certain hour. Nikos would wait until it was time to go in, and he would follow the crowd to the healing hot springs that were fast becoming packed with all kinds of seekers, young, old, rich, poor, naughty, nice, etc. Nikos would allow his mind to drink in the healing as he did further meditations and asked Apollo, the sun god, as well as the father of Asclepius, to forgive him of all iniquities (even the ones he doesn't recall).

After a long wait of dipping in the hot springs and meditating, a white robed "therapeutic" would escort Nikos to the *enkoimeteria,* a big sleeping hall where they spent the night and dream healing would occur. The incubation chamber was filled with stone beds in small enclaves removed from sound, traffic, and any other disturbance. When communicating with Asclepius, it was essential you be removed from any kind of distractions, so silence was golden in these dimly lit incubation chambers.

Nikos would lie on the stone bed, covered by a blanket that was also white, and as he fell into sleep, would beseech Asclepius to heal him of a certain malady. Asclepius would then arrive in deep dreamscape, perhaps accompanied by one of his daughters or sons (there were six), a dwarf, or—most importantly—a cock, a snake, or a dog. Any kind of contact from the animals such as a touch, a lick or a kiss of healing signaled that the request had been answered. However, on occasion Asclepius would do a sort of spiritual bargaining.

Quite often, Asclepius would say that he would remove the malady, but until the emotional issue was overcome that caused the original ill, there would be another lesser problem to take its place. Perhaps you implored Asclepius to remove your asthma, and he did, but, until you stopped beating the crap out of your kids, you would have crummy eyesight. If you stopped terrorizing your family, your eyes would also correct themselves and you would be completely healed.

In time, you would be awoken by your therapeutic, who would take you outside to the olive grove, and there discuss your sacred dream. Later, after days or weeks elapsed, you would come back to Epidaurus and leave an offering for Asclepius to thank him for the catharsis. Ancients often left a wax votive in the shape of the part of the anatomy that had been healed, animal sacrifices, or another memento to pay homage for the miraculous healing event. In ancient records, there was an elderly bald man who came to ask Asclepius to grow his hair back. The other ancients thought this was a ridiculous request and mocked him for such a waste of the god's time. Well, not only did a full crop of hair grow back, it was thick and curly—even better than before! Obviously the healer had compassion for the seeker and knew how much his hair meant to him.

There is a spectacular museum on the grounds of Epidaurus with many of the thousands of votive, statues, columns, and other relics from this stellar temple that you can find online. This is important to show that there were thousands of recorded healings taking place; moreover, so grateful were the seekers that they actually donated enough money to build one of the world's most prestigious amphitheaters, right there on temple grounds. Built in the fourth century BC, the Romans later extended it to seat fifteen thousand people. It's still used today.

The view of the Peloponnesian landscape was an integral part of the design for Greek theatres (not Roman ones), since the theatre itself was considered cathartic through the performance of Greek tragedies. These were a form of therapy in ancient days, since you released your own pain while watching the dramatic performances. What makes this amphitheater such a marvel are the acoustics. An actor needs no amplification to be heard in the furthest stretches of the audience, and today tour guides love to have their groups scatter in the stands and strike a match to show how easily even such a gentle sound can be heard.

Asclepius can be invoked for any form of healing, and if a "dream lick" occurs, one can count on a miraculous recovery.

Ancient Asclepiad Prayer:

> "Great Asklepios, skilled to heal mankind, all-ruling, and physician kind; whose arts medicinal can alone assuage diseases dire, and stop their dreadful rage. Strong, lenient God, regard my suppliant prayer, bring gentle health, adorned with lovely hair; convey the means of mitigating pain, and raging deadly pestilence restrain. O power

all-flourishing, abundant, bright, Apollo's honored offspring, God of light; husband of blameless Hygeia (Health), the constant foe of dread disease, the minister of woe: come, blessed savior, human health defend, and to the mortal life afford a prosperous end." Amen.

Please see my video on YouTube, and search for:

**Dream Healing with Asklepios
the Ancient Barefoot Healer**
or
Epidaurus and the Sanctuary of Asclepius

"Let Christ into your heart, give him a loving welcome home and then...he has to pay you rent."

Saint Bernadette

CHAPTER 9
Saint Bernadette

On one occasion when she had finally escaped the crowds
by taking refuge in a sympathetic neighbor's house, she
crept home in the dark to her bed, answering her mother's
query as to how she felt with a sigh,
'I'm worn out with all that kissing.'

Born January 7, 1844, into extreme poverty in Lourdes,
France, Bernadette's family were so poor they made
their home in a one room underground abandoned jail
cell they referred to as the "the dungeon." Home to six kids
and two parents, the cell made for what one would assume
was a chaotic household, yet neighbors were often impressed
at the calm, polite, and gentle nature of the family.

On February 11, 1858, while gathering firewood with her
sister and a friend, Bernadette had to stop to find a way to
cross a ravine that ran in front of the grotto. Not wanting
to get her stockings wet, she sat on a rock to take them off.
Suddenly, she saw a rose and heard a rushing wind—though,
oddly, nothing moved. She looked deeper into the grotto

to see a dazzling white light, and inside of it a small, beautiful lady appeared who stood upon a bouquet of golden roses. Bernadette did not know why this strange apparition appeared, and had no idea who the lady was—and at the time she did not connect this to the Virgin Mother. Her sister and friend came back to find her, but saw nothing.

Three days later Bernadette returned to the grotto with her sister and several girlfriends, and upon approach to the grotto, feeling compelled, she knelt down to pray. The beautiful lady appeared again as Bernadette went into a trance while praying, smiling and oblivious to anything around her. Frightened for her safety, the friends threw holy water and a giant rock at the alleged vision, causing it to disappear. Rejoicing in the "killing" of this weird thing, Bernadette came back into awareness—but now in a state of horrified shock that her friends could be so disrespectful.

Bernadette now returned alone to the grotto to find the beautiful lady again on February 18, and when she appeared, she spoke to Bernadette and asked her to return every day for the next fortnight (fourteen days). This caused a great commotion in the town, as her parents forbade her from going to the grotto due to the public humiliation. Bernadette defied anyone who tried to stop her, and was even brought to the police station, where the police commissioner, as well as the district attorney, threated to "put her in jail" for these alleged delusions. Bernadette righteously answered, "Put me in jail? That is like home to me. Finally I will have my own room!"

Authorities were forced to back down since no crime was actually committed, so they let the kid walk. She caused such an uproar in the community, however, it divided the town. Half insisted she was a lunatic and demanded she be put in an asylum, while the other half believed something miraculous was actually going on. Whatever they believed, huge throngs of townsfolk followed her, and it became like a circus show, with some muttering prayers while others hooted and hollered at the spectacle. Imagine their incredulity when, on one of her daily pilgrimages, she went into a completely altered state, clawed at the muddy ground then kissed it, plucked and gobbled blades of grass, rubbed mud all over her face, and then, in a grand finale to the show, began to swallow the mud. The entire crowd was so disturbed, even her most devout followers thought maybe it was true that she had gone insane. The townsfolk stared, silent, at the bizarre spectacle unfolding before them.

The very next day, to everyone's shock, the grotto was no longer surrounded by a muddy clump but a spectacular place that flowed with pure, clean water. A miracle had indeed occurred, and people got down on their knees and asked the Holy Mother for forgiveness for their disbelief in her and their sweet Bernadette.

The Holy Mother appeared to Bernadette for the next few days and told her a chapel should be built near the grotto for people to pray and be healed. Bernadette told the still skeptical priests who insisted they wanted proof the lady

was real that the Holy Mother told her to tell the priests she was the "Immaculate Conception," and even the most negative now knew Bernadette did indeed have a connection to the Holy Mother since those were the same words spoken secretly by the Pope just a few days before. The chapel was built, and there have since been hundreds of documented, scientifically confirmed healings.

Bernadette was an abstract thinker, and besides being canonized a Saint, has also been elevated to the rare status of a Christian Mystic (due to her ecstatic visions with the Holy Mother), and her body still lies incorrupt at the church at Lourdes. Interestingly, the church only discovered upon exhuming her corpse some seventy-five years later, that this miracle had even occurred. When her tomb was opened, they found Bernadette exactly as she had been on her death. Her hands still held the rosary and the crucifix, which were both decaying.

Dr. Jourdan, the surgeon who was present for the exhumation, left a written record in the community archives describing what transpired:

> The coffin was opened in the presence of the Bishop of Nevers, the mayors of the town several canons and ourselves. We noticed no smell. The body was clothed in the habit of Bernadette's order. The habit was damp. Only the face, hands and forearms were uncovered.
>
> The head was tilted to the left. The face was dull white. The mouth was open slightly and it could be seen that the teeth were still in place. The hands, which were crossed upon the breast, were perfectly preserved, as were the nails. The hands still held a rusting Rosary. The veins on the forearms stood out.
>
> After the identification, the Sisters washed the body and dressed it in a fresh habit. It was then placed in a new coffin lined with white silk, and lowered back into the tomb. The entire process was completed at half past five in the evening.
>
> On 13 August 1913, Pope Pius X authorized the introduction of the Cause for Canonization—Bernadette could now be given the title 'Venerable'. This meant that body had to be exhumed once again. This process was interrupted by the war, and the body was not re-exhumed until 3 April 1919. The process was the same as before—as were the results. The body remained intact.

Saint Bernadette used to say "Life is only heaven's waiting room," and at the age of thirty-five she no longer had to stand in line. Her short life impacted history forever, as between five and eight million people a year visit Lourdes, in the hope that the "beautiful lady" she once saw will also help them too. If you would like to have a prayer inserted at the grotto in Lourdes, go to www.Lourdes-france.org; here you can insert your petition and have the nuns pray for your appeal directly to the Holy Mother.

Our Lady of Lourdes Novena

Be blessed, O most pure Virgin, for having vouch-safed to manifest your shining with life, sweetness and beauty, in the Grotto of Lourdes, saying to the child, St. Bernadette: "I am the Immaculate Conception." A thousand times we congratulate you upon your Immaculate Conception. And now, O ever Immaculate Virgin, Mother of mercy, Health of the sick, Refuge of sinners, Comforter of the afflicted, you know our wants, our troubles, our sufferings deign to cast upon us a look of mercy.

By appearing in the Grotto of Lourdes, you were pleased to make it a privileged sanctuary, whence you dispense your favors, and already many have obtained the cure of their infirmities, both spiritual and physical. We come, therefore, with the most unbounded confidence to implore your maternal intercession. Obtain for us, O loving Mother, the granting of our request. (state your request)
Through gratitude for your favors, we will endeavor to imitate your virtues, that we may one day share your glory.
Our Lady of Lourdes, Mother of Christ, you had influence with your divine son while upon earth. You have the same influence now in Heaven. Pray

for us; obtain for us from your Divine Son our special requests if it be the Divine Will. Amen.
Our Lady of Lourdes, pray for us. Saint Bernadette, pray for us.

* * *

I Am Bernadette was a book written by this most enigmatic saint, where you can listen to her inspirational thoughts on life, God, and the healing power of prayer.
Novena (say for nine straight days) or Petition to St. Bernadette:

"Dear Saint Bernadette, Chosen by Almighty God as a channel of His Graces and Blessings, and through your humble obedience to the requests of Our Blessed Mother, Mary, you gained for us the Miraculous waters of Spiritual and physical healing. We implore you to listen to our pleading prayers that we may be healed of our Spiritual and physical imperfections.
Place our petitions in the Hands of our Holy Mother, Mary, so that She may place them at the feet of Her beloved Son, Our Lord and Savior Jesus Christ, that He may look on us with mercy and compassion: (Make Petition)
Help, O Dear Saint Bernadette to follow your example, so that irrespective of our own pain and suffering we may always be mindful of the needs of others, especially those whose sufferings are greater than ours. As we await the Mercy of God, remind us to offer up our pain and suffering for the conversion of sinners, and in reparation for the sins and blasphemies of mankind.

Pray for Saint Bernadette, that like you, we may always be obedient to the will of Our Heavenly Father, and that through our prayers and humility we may bring consolation to the Most Sacred Heart of Jesus and the Immaculate Heart of Mary that have been so grievously wounded by our sins. Holy Saint Bernadette of Lourdes, Pray for us." Amen.

On YouTube, search for:

True History of Lourdes & St Bernadette Excerpt 3
or
St. Bernadette's Incorrupt Body

"Sorry is not enough. You need to fix it."

The Archangel Raguel upon my feeble apology.

CHAPTER 10

The Archangel Raguel

His name means "friend of God," and he is invoked for disputes, defending the underdog, problems in the family, orderliness, and anything where arbitration is concerned.

Raguel ranks at the higher order and is said to be the one who rules all the angels and archangels in Heaven, and makes sure they work together in perfect harmony. It is also said he is a warm and friendly angel, but this, I can assure you, he is not. He's more of a cool angel, and I like him more for not being some sop that runs around strumming a harp and spinning his halo (to be honest, none of the angels are the goody-two-shoes like we are taught. Righteous, tough, and sometimes cold, angels are more real than we could ever imagine). I cannot say I am proud of my encounter with Raguel, which occurred in my mid-twenties, but he left a huge impression on my life. Let me explain.

While we were living in London, my husband would get up at seven a.m. and go to work, while I tend to awake around four a.m. This created a disruption for us both, so I started sleeping in the back room, a tranquil place that looked over beautiful gardens. I slept in a French bed that I bought at an antique shop near Winston Churchill's estate in a very old village. It has a lot of energy in it and was built around 1880. I bring this up because it has powerful energy that enhances whatever happens when I sleep, so I'd usually awaken with great peace. So it was a shock to awaken with a spirit choking me around the neck in the middle of the night.

I commanded it to leave—in the name of God of course—and felt it instantly begin to fly away. I say "fly" because it didn't disappear like other souls, and it seemed to go up and out. This tells me it's an earthbound spirit on the hunt for trouble. I immediately had a great idea: I would use this dirty, rotten scoundrel to get a dirty, rotten deed done!

"Spirit! Come back!" I shrieked, "I know someone you can really give it to!" I immediately sensed the presence back in the room. I could tell the spirit was curious over my lack of fear. I thought of this guy who was causing my husband great distress at work, not to mention every other human being he came into contact with. My husband was actually his boss, quit his job, and this man was outraged to not have his protective wing around him. Since they both still worked in the same building, he would go out of his way to cause my husband harm and disruption. Once I went to a class to learn how to relax and five of the seven people attending (including his own mother!) were there because they were so distressed by this one man. The spirit waited to hear what I had to say.

"Go to Shane's house," I said aloud. "Feel free to scare the living crap out of him!" I visualized the image of Shane in my head to let the spirit know exactly who to look for. I was proud of myself—until the next day.

I was in class at the London College of Psychic Studies, and my elderly teacher was asking us if we'd had any psychic phenomena occur that past week. I raised my hand and proudly told her about the bad spirit, and how I turned this bad event into a really good thing.

She gazed at me serenely, but her wise old eyes turned to horror when she heard me speak. She said, to my dismay, "*You did what?* My dear, you are not being trained to be a witch! What happened to your ethics? You need a special class just in that!" I was crushed she didn't share in my love for standing up to that evil spirit and then using it to throttle that rotten troublemaker Shane. Later that night, things got even worse after I went to bed.

I went out of my body and landed in an old office with a hefty Italian lady sitting at a desk in a white uniform. Speaking in Italian (no, I don't speak it) she said, "You are very lucky because today you are going to meet an angel!" I was ecstatic. Finally I'd get some credit for my quick thinking and brilliant idea from this angel for how I handled the bad soul!

I felt a tap on my shoulder and turned around. There was a barefoot man with long, curly brown hair, a big felt fedora, an old white V-neck t-shirt and beat up jeans. I asked him excitedly, "Are you taking me to see the angel?"

His lids lowered as he calmly replied, "I am the angel."

Startled, I stood up. The room turned to light as I stood before him, really having a hard time accepting this was a supersonic being—since he was nothing like what I was taught about in all those years at Catholic school. I mean, where were the wings? The halo? The sweet disposition?

"I am Raguel," he said.

"Raphael?" I asked.

"No, Raguel," he patiently replied.

"Raziel?" I asked, still not sure I'd hear him right.

"No, Raguel," he calmly said again.

I'd never heard his name before and said, "Raguel? You mean, like the spaghetti sauce?"

Why he didn't strike me down with lightning bolts or leprosy I will never know, but I could tell he was not in the mood to interact with some random piece of earth debris.

"You are in *big trouble*," he said, and I'm sure I looked startled as he continued, "for what you sent on Shane."

I was reeling that all this was about that, and realizing it must have been a really bad choice since an angel would never lie, I mechanically uttered, "Oh, I'm really sorry about that."

The angel's next words made my blood run cold as he slowly replied with a look of fury in his eyes, "*Sorry is not enough.*"

I didn't know what to do and was waiting for a trap door to drop me down to a fiery vault when he also said, "You created this problem, *so now you need to fix it.*"

"How?" I asked, mystified.

"*Get him help.*" The angel apparently couldn't take me anymore and vaporized himself.

I awoke in my body. "Oh great," I wondered "How the bloody hell am I supposed to do that?" I put my horns together and began to think.

I asked my husband's mother, who was a nurse, what I could do to help him since "Shane has gone insane, or bonkers as you say here across the pond." My husband's mom took charge and called in some psychiatric counselors, and they went out to his remote ranch to find him in a field with a bottle of whiskey and a shotgun.

To make a long story short, Shane got the help he needed—and even though the rest of us had to contend with him for years, Raguel was right. I was wrong to interfere with another's actions, even though at the time I hatched my plot it seemed innocent enough—having no idea the bad spirit pushed him so close to the edge. It made me wonder how many times we have caused trouble without even knowing what we did. I had no idea, and yet, somehow, I was still responsible for the reactions. Years later I saw Shane at a party, and he thanked me for asking my husband's mom to help him. He went onto to get a gorgeous wife and three kids and retired young to his dream dairy farm. Somehow God had blessed his life, and he seemed like a new man.

Moral of the Story: Never wish ill on another—no matter how despicable they are.

Prayer to Raguel:
'You are Raguel, Friend of God,
You are Raguel, Angel of Earth,
You are Raguel who stands guard over the Heavenly Host,
Angel of Principalities, Guard of Heaven, we honor your name.
Please help me dissolve any altercations with (name subject, person).Thank you for helping me do the right thing Archangel Raguel.'

If you ever start to lose your soul like Shane did,
please go to YouTube and watch my video:

Soul Retrieval.

"I can remove any obstacle in your life."

Sweet Ganesh (6,0000 + years old)

CHAPTER 11

Ganesh

Remover of Obstacles

Sweet, gentle Ganesh was the first god known to man in the first religion on Earth—Hinduism. The way an elephant clears tall grass and creates a trail one can follow, so, too, does sweet Ganesh clear the way, removing any obstacle in life. Divinatory scholars suggest Ganesh was man's early interpretation of Michael the Archangel since they possess similar attributes. I cannot fathom this connection, since I count on both to help me out in totally different situations. Ganesh has a gentle energy like a cuddly dog, whereas Michael appears as a warrior. The only common denominator between the two is they are both powerful, and funnel the energy of protection.

Ganesh has an energy we immediately feel drawn to. Hinduism comes from the oldest religion known to man, swirled from the river in northern India known as the Sindhu, but the Persians called them "Hindus," and the name just stuck. In a nutshell, Hinduism has sprawling folklore, complicated rituals, vast literature, and opulent art that says to the world, "You can have what you want. The world is awash with sensual pleasures and beauty— go get it: but seek it intelligently!"

Hindu scholars, however, say the sole pursuit of the Path of Desire fails for four reasons:

1. Wealth, fame, and power do not reproduce when shared, and cannot be distributed without diminishing one's own portion.
2. Drive for success is insatiable. The Buddhists have a term called "hungry ghost", which means absolutely nothing will satiate this type of being, in this life or in the next.
3. Worldly success centers meaning on the self (like hedonism), which proves too small for perpetual enthusiasm.
4. Wealth, fame, and power do not survive death because you cannot take it with you when you go.

Hindus think the Path of Desire leads to disillusion, whereas the Path of Renunciation makes life more meaningful and strengthens the life force. In addition, we must listen to the multitudes who followed the Path of Desire but, in the end, found only futility and despair.

In the west, we relate events to chronological and biological age. Hinduism goes one step further and also covers multiple life spans (reincarnation). That's why some like to play cops and robbers all their life, while others find it paltry (young and old souls). On the path of renunciation, two transcendental thoughts emerge:

1. Serving the self leads to boredom.
2. Do your best in whatever you do; give 100 percent commitment.

In actuality what we want is
1. infinite being
2. infinite knowledge
3. infinite bliss

Hindus believe we already possess these, and what we really want is "moksha," or liberation from the finite. The ultimate center of you beyond the scope of your personality is the hidden self, known as the "atman." The godhead self they call the "Brahman." The three distractions we have that keep us from those inner treasures are

1. physical pain
2. frustration
3. boredom

Detachment from the self thus becomes key, because the Hindus see the mind as holding hidden continents stretching to infinity. The also believed there are four paths to God:

1. knowledge
2. love
3. work
4. yoga (ancients believed it created an integration of the mind).

Oddly enough, 6,400 years later Carl Jung used this same model but used different buzz words:

1. reflective
2. emotional
3. active
4. experimental

With this knowledge, the Hindus had a strong belief in karma, which can be thought of as a moral law of cause and effect. To help us on our way through this voyage in the physical world, the Hindus believed in nine levels of God (that reminds me of the nine choirs of angels), that were put in place to help us, and they rank in descending order as follows:

1. Ganesh–Annapurna–Maya
2. Balrama–Garuda–Ram
3. Bhuvaneshwari–Hanuman–Saraswati
4. Brahma–Indra–Shakti
5. Buddito–Kali–Shiva
6. Dhanwantari–Kartikau–Sita
7. Dhumvati–Krishna–Vaman
8. Durga–Kurma–Vishnu
9. Ganga–Lakshmi–Matangi

I do not wish to overwhelm you with too many facts, but it's important to see our beloved elephant Lord Ganesh has a rich history, and was not a trinket a bored sword thrower concocted. According to Hindu legend, he was the young son of two great Hindu Gods, Parvati and Shiva. Unaware, Shiva accidently cut of his young son's head, and becoming so enraged by the accident, Parvati threatened to destroy the earth and heavens. To quell her sorrow, Shiva sent out his celestial squadrons to find the first creature with his eyes facing north (direction associated with wisdom), and instructed them to bring back his head. They found an elephant snoozing by the riverbank, amputated his head and upon reception, Shiva transplanted it upon his son's shoulders. Parvati was ecstatic to have the pachyderm as her son.

Ganesh winds into our DNA and collective unconscious, since he's been with us since the dawn of time. This alone makes him a potent ally whom all of us have heard of through multiple lifetimes on this planet. Christianity is a little over

2,000 years old, making Hinduism 4,500 years older. Does this mean all those people for so many millenniums who led pious lives are all going to burn in hell since they worshipped an elephant instead of a man? It's all the same thing. Energy comes cloaked in different guises, so you may as well use the most powerful one to tap into your unconscious mind to remove any obstacles and create the most spectacular luck. Invoke Ganesh whenever you hit a wall and watch how the bricks miraculously crumble.

If you feel let down by people, turn toward Ganesh. Our defenses go down with an animal, making it our secret weapon as we go through this obstacle course called life.

Prayer to Sweet Ganesh:
"Salutations to the supreme Lord Ganesha, whose curved trunk (vakra-tunda) and massive body (maha-kaayaa) shines like a million suns (surya-koti) and showers his blessings on everyone (sama-prabhaa). Oh my lord of lords Ganesha (kurume-deva), kindly remove all obstacles (nir-vighnam), always (sarva-) and forever (sarvadaa-) from all my activities and endeavors (sarva-kaaryeshu). Thank you Lord Ganesh, for removing this particular obstacle (name issue) from my life." Amen.

You can also say:
"Please help remove (name obstacle) from my life. Thank you for your help, Sweet Ganesh, it's much better now."

To hear the Angel of Song sing an ancient chant to our dear Ganesh, go to YouTube and search:

Six-Thousand-Year-Old Chant to Remove Obstacles in Your Life

"I believe that everything happens for a reason.
People change so that you can learn to let go, things
go wrong so that you appreciate them when they're
right, you believe lies so you eventually learn to trust
no one but yourself, and sometimes good things fall
apart so better things can fall together."

Marilyn Monroe (1926-1962)

CHAPTER 12
Marilyn Monroe

"Hollywood is a place where they'll pay you a thousand dollars
for a kiss and fifty cents for your soul."
Marilyn Monroe

know this blonde beauty isn't one we think of as a spirit
helper. I didn't either, until the night she came into my out–
of-body destination. I was going through a grieving phase
after my father committed suicide and living in gray, rainy
London at the time. One night when I went to sleep I left my
body and found myself on the sidelines of an empty, muddy
dog track. I had never been to a dog track in my life, and
certainly had no desire whatsoever to visit one, and yet there
I was. I stood in the gloom, wondering why I was there as a
pretty blonde woman came toward me wearing clam digger
pants, a white blouse, and a pink sweater wrapped around
her shoulders, and I watched as she navigated through the
mud in her dainty pink flat shoes. She looked familiar, and I
realized it was the actress Marilyn Monroe. I had never seen

any of her films before and wondered why on earth her spirit would want to talk to me.

She stood right before me, gazing at me with the prettiest blue eyes. I was expecting her to be laughing and having fun, but in fact she was quite serious as she began to speak. There were no introductions or pleasantries, she got right down to brass tacks and this is what she said, "You are letting things in life get on top of you. Everything you've ever had that was bad you need to use—like I did. Take all the bad experiences and let them push you forward from behind, not crush you from the top. You need to use that bad energy to make you fly."

I answered, "You mean like booster rockets on a spaceship?"

She looked at me like I was speaking Chinese and then disappeared. I looked toward the track and knew it was time to go back to my body. When I awoke I did as she said and her message completely altered my world. It gave me a new perspective on using sorrow and pain to your advantage, and even though the pain was still there, it had no power over me—I was free.

A little thought to send to Heaven:

"Help me convert my pain to push me forward, Marilyn. Thanks for all your help. I agree, we need to use all energy to boost us forward, not crush us from on top. Thank you for your wisdom, Marilyn, it has helped me."

If you want to go back to "the day," and be inspired by Marilyn, go to YouTube and search:

**Marilyn Monroe -
Diamonds Are A Girl's Best Friend**
It will make you smile.

*"After my death I will do more. My real mission
will begin after my death."*

Padre Pio (May 25, 1887–September 23, 1968)

CHAPTER 13

Saint Padre Pio

On June 16, 2002, Pope John Paul II canonized Padre Pio of Pietrelcina, one of the greatest miracle workers of all times. He didn't heal hundreds—he healed thousands. He could "read" souls, he often was seen levitating, he bore the stigmata for fifty years and lost one cup of blood a day (but it never got infected, though it caused great pain and embarrassment for the kind priest who covered it with gloves), he was often recorded bi-locating (appearing far from where he was), he always smelled like flowers (called the "odor of sanctity"), he understood all languages, his face often transfigured into Christ while conducting Consecration of the Holy Eucharist in mass, and some of his more dramatic, scientifically documented incidents included a worker who lost an eye *that later materialized under the bandages in the hospital* after Pio visited him in a bilocation, and whose shattered face was suddenly healed. In Italy more people now pray to Padre Pio than to Jesus Christ.

It had been a long day in the confessional booth for Padre Pio. Sleeping on average only three hours, conducting multiple masses and spending up to sixteen hours a day listening to confessions, Padre Pio was a dedicated priest in the church of San Giovanni Rotondo, in Puglia, southern Italy. It was 1947, the little girl confessing was seven years old, and her grandmother, already done with her session, waited for the small child in the back of the church. Little Gemma De Giorgio came walking back towards her grandma but then stopped and turned to go back to the confessional—she had forgotten to confess one more sin.

Padre Pio had finally finished his long day and had just stepped out of the confessional booth when the little girl ran smack-dab into him. Startled, the grandmother apologized that the little girl was not trying to be disrespectful; the fact was the little girl was blind. "She was born with no pupils," her grandmother explained.

Padre Pio, well known for doing more miracles than any other mortal aside from Saint Francis of Assisi, began to speak. "Can you promise that you and your grandchild will not weep when she sees things on the drive home today?" Even the blind child felt something critical in the request by the imminent priest. They choked back tears as Padre placed his hands upon her eyes and went into an altered state. When he was done the child was still blind, but on the drive home she shocked her grandma and the other relatives in the car when she started shouting she could see the boats on the sea! Everyone held back tears and began to give thanks and pray—this was a most miraculous day.

There are multitudes of miracles attributed to Padre Pio, too numerous to mention, as compelling as the blind child and even more remarkable. There was one, though, that stands out for its supernatural qualities, witnessed by many of the allied forces in World War II, referred to as the "Sky

Incident." Author of *Padre Pio: The True Story*, C. Bernard Ruffin, recounts:

"There are many stories concerning allied pilots who attempted to bomb San Giovanni but were stopped by an apparition of a 'monk' standing in the air with his arms outstretched," says Ruffin. "There are fliers who swore that they had sighted a figure in the sky, sometimes normal size, sometimes gigantic, usually in the form of a monk or priest. The sightings were too frequent and the reports came from too many sources to be totally discounted. Several people from Foggia, where thousands were killed in the air raids, said that a bomb, falling into a room where they had huddled, landed near a photograph of Padre Pio. They claimed that when it exploded, it 'burst like a soap bubble.' Others reported that while bombs were raining down upon the city, they cried, 'Padre Pio, you have to save us!' While they were speaking, a bomb fell into their midst, but did not explode."

Bernardo Rosini, a general of the Italian Air Force, told a story: "At Bari was located the general command of the U.S. Air Force. I know several officers who told me of having been saved by Padre Pio during air missions."

"One day," General Rosini continued, "an American commander wanted to lead a squadron of bombers himself to destroy the German arms depository of war material that was located at San Giovanni Rotondo. The commander related that as he approached the target, he and his pilots saw rising in the sky the figure of a friar with his hands held outward. The bombs released of their own accord, falling in the woods, and the planes completely reversed course without any intervention by the pilots."

Someone told the commanding general that in a convent at this little town of San Giovanni Rotondo, there lived a saintly man, a friar known for sanctity. At war's end, the general wanted to go meet this person. "He was accompanied by several pilots," Rosini continued. "He went to the convent of the Capuchins. As soon as he crossed the threshold of the sacristy, he found himself in front of several friars, among whom he immediately recognized the one who had 'stopped' his planes. Padre Pio stepped forward to meet him, and putting his hand on his shoulder, he said, 'So, you're the one who wanted to get rid of us all!'"

Padre Pio himself went through many attacks and torments by the devil, often screams and moans were heard coming from his quarters and loud bangs and thuds accompanied them. Pio also had visions, even as a small boy of the Virgin Mary, Jesus, his own Guardian Angel- but as he got older and closer to God these visions also brought with them sinister forces. Pio could always differentiate between the authentic God and the illusions of the devil as he reflected on one particularly dark event that occurred on August 5th, 1918:

"While I was hearing the boys' confessions on the evening of the 5th [August] I was suddenly terrorized by the sight of a celestial person who presented himself to my mind's eye. He had in his hand a sort of weapon like a very long sharp-pointed steel blade which seemed to emit fire. At the very instant that I saw all this, I saw that person hurl the weapon into my soul with all his might. I cried out with difficulty and felt I was dying. I asked the boy to leave because I felt ill and no longer had the strength to continue. This agony lasted uninterruptedly until the morning of the 7th. I cannot tell you how much I suffered during this period of anguish. Even my entrails were torn and ruptured by the weapon, and nothing was spared. From that day on I have been mortally wounded. I feel in the depths of my soul a wound that is always open and which causes me continual agony."

Padre Pio had physical wounds from many brutal assaults by his visions, and when they leave behind scars and pain they become known as a "transverberation", which makes the recipient much closer to God. Lasting up to 10 weeks and nearly putting people over the edge, when finished they are followed by intense peace and tranquility.

Padre Pio was looking forward to dying in order to do more good acts for people all around the world. Since his death he has provided spiritual intercession for many and can be called upon in times of trouble for any kind of healing, even for lost hope and causes science cannot help anymore. In his confessional booth, Pio often conducted these healings, where little, if any, physical contact was made but he always asked the seeker one question that he insisted they answer aloud, "What underlying source do you think has caused you this pain?" So, when you ask him to help you, speak aloud the reason you may have gotten this issue- even if you have to guess- and always remember his famous quote;

"Pray, hope, and don't worry. Worry is useless. God is merciful and will hear your prayers."

Invocation for Intercession from Saint Padre Pio:

Beloved Padre Pio, today I come to add my prayer to the thousands of prayers offered to you every day by those who love and venerate you. They ask for cures and healings, earthly and spiritual blessings, and peace for body and mind. And because of your friendship with the Lord, he heals those you ask to be healed, and forgives those you forgive.

Through your visible wounds of the Cross, which you bore for 50 years, you were chosen in our time to glorify the crucified Jesus. Because the Cross has been replaced by other symbols, please help us to bring it back in our midst, for we acknowledge it is the only true sign of salvation.

As we lovingly recall the wounds that pierced your hands, feet and side, we not only remember the blood you shed in pain, but your smile, and the invisible halo of sweet smelling flowers that surrounded your presence, the perfume of sanctity.

Padre Pio, may the healings of the sick become the testimony that the Lord has invited you to join the holy company of Saints. In your kindness, please help me with my own special request: (mention here your petition, and make the sign of the Cross). Bless me and my loved ones. In the name of the Father, the Son and the Holy Spirit. Amen

It was only recently discovered in 2008, upon exhumation, that Padre Pio was incorrupt. Go to YouTube and search for:

A Tribute to Padre Pio

If you go to YouTube you can also see an older Gemma—still with no pupils—recounting her story on YouTube, although it's all spoken in Italian; and yes, she has perfect vision, although her eyes do have an unusual appearance.

Gemma and Padre Pio

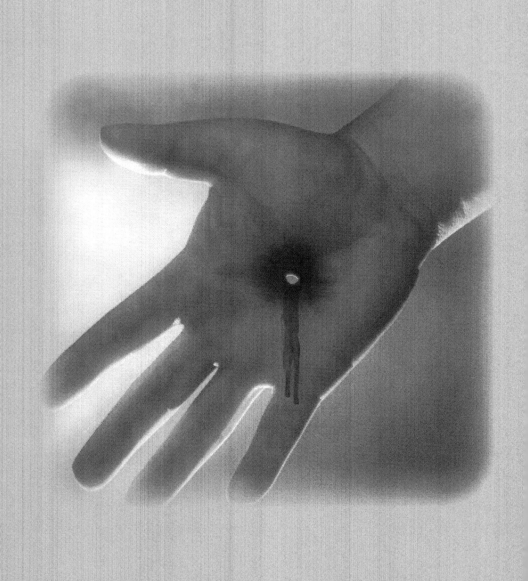

CHAPTER 14

What Is the Stigmata?

S tigmata are painful marks and lacerations, indigenous to members of the Roman Catholic Church, particularly those who are of strict religious orders, such as a nun or priest, and to date there are sixty-two recorded cases that have occurred since 1200 AD. These wounds corroborate precisely with the crucifixion wounds of Jesus Christ, such as the hands, feet, open gash on the side, crown of thorns, scourges on the back, and, in some cases, rope marks on the wrist, and, as was the case with the first stigmatic St. Francis, giant six-inch nail marks that *actually extend beyond the mutilated flesh* near the bleeding ulcers. There are also several recorded stigmatas where blood poured out of the eyes.

Causing the bearer cruel rejection and suspicion before wounds are authenticated, the stigmata tends to be so shocking people cannot believe it's for real. In many instances, the holy member was kept in a sort of lock-down where they were watched and followed intensely, so members around them could eventually see they were not inflicting the wounds upon themselves.

Studied for over a millennium by the medical community of its time, no doctor or research group has ever been able to explain the cause of a genuine stigmata. It defies analysis, especially in the fact that it never becomes infected, and gives off a delicate fragrance referred to as "the odor of sanctity." In some instances, as was the case of the last stigmatic, Padre Pio, who died in 1969, one cup of blood was lost each day for over fifty years. Despite relatively modern science, x-rays, and research done to try and explain it in further detail, even multiple twentieth century doctors reported the event far beyond scientific evaluation. One strange symptom of the stigmata is that it causes the bearer to desperately crave the Holy Eucharist. The Holy Eucharist represents the body of Jesus Christ, and perhaps the energy from this holy wafer somehow replenishes that lost portion and physical debility the stigmata causes. Many stigmatics had recurring bleeding that stops and starts after receiving Holy Communion. Most of the stigmatics also exhibit a condition known as *inedia*, where the bearer lives with minimal food or water for inordinate amounts of time, except for the Holy Eucharist, causing them to become extremely underweight.

There are actually two kinds of stigmata, physical and spiritual. Physical stigmata is the clearly seen type that shocks the observer, while spiritual stigmata is the brutal pain suffered by the stigmatic without signs seen by the common man. Many sufferers pleaded and prayed to God to have the invisible spiritual stigmata because the ridicule of the public brought unwanted attention to them, getting in the way of their holy focus. When proven genuine, they were then forced to deal with a mesmerized public who still could not think on anything but the blood. Stigmata sufferers were scrutinized either way with the public, and although they had no problem bearing the pain, they despised the attention it garnered.

Sometimes God would answer their prayers and allow their wounds to become invisible, though still pain-riddled, and this helped the bearer to deal with the public humiliation. Often the skeptics came from their own inner circles, and this potential betrayal of trust caused them great sadness and consternation.

One thought provoking report made by a biographer in 1230 about Saint Francis, Thomas of Celano, in the book *First Life of St. Francis*, states:

> When the blessed servant of God saw these things he was filled with wonder, but he did not know what the vision meant. He rejoiced greatly in the benign and gracious expression with which he saw himself regarded by the seraph, whose beauty was indescribable; yet he was alarmed by the fact that the seraph was affixed to the cross and was suffering terribly. Thus Francis rose, one might say, sad and happy, joy and grief alternating in him. He wondered anxiously what this vision could mean, and his soul was uneasy as it searched for understanding. And as his understanding sought in vain for an explanation and his heart was filled with perplexity at the great novelty of this vision, the marks of nails began to appear in his hands and feet, just as he had seen them slightly earlier in the crucified man above him. His wrists and feet seemed to be pierced by nails, with the heads of the nails appearing on his wrists and on the upper sides of his feet, the points appearing on the other side. The marks were round on the palm of each hand but elongated on the other side, and small pieces of flesh jutting out from the rest took on the appearance of the nail-ends, bent and driven back. In the same way the marks of nails were impressed

on his feet and projected beyond the rest of the flesh. Moreover, his right side had a large wound as if it had been pierced with a spear, and it often bled so that his tunic and trousers were soaked with his sacred blood.

Once the stigmata appeared, the bearer was put into a lifetime of pain.

To watch and learn a little more about this mystery as described by priests, professors, scientists, and doctors, please go to YouTube and search:

Mysteries - Stigmata PT 1 of 2
or
Mysteries - Stigmata PT 2 of 2

"Know that I love you, Tristan. Wherever you go, whatever you see, I will always be with you."

Isolde the Ascended Master

CHAPTER 15

Isolde

A Celtic princess invoked for issues of love, healing from divorce or breakup, reigniting passion, unrequited love, those in search of their soul mate and even the lovelorn can all benefit from her astonishing powers. Compared to other ascended beings, Isolde is incredibly accessible and will help you magnetize that elusive blessing of love—even if you lead the loneliest of lives.

Isolde was a Celtic princess who lived in Ireland where her parents ruled as king and queen. She fell madly in love with Tristan from Cornwall, but, according to conflicting legends with the same theme, they could only be together in death because life cruelly tore them apart. Isolde underwent the pain we have all felt, and today tries to help any who ask her for support, and she does the job fast—*but only if you are open to receiving it.*

Inspired by their great love, this connection speaks loudly through the ages, since many of us have wondered if there's anybody really out there we're meant to share our life with.

We tend to close down and delude ourselves that we're better off alone—and sure, we can weather the tough times, but the true test occurs when we're *happy* and want to share our joy with someone we love. We look around and it hits us that there's no one there—and our own triumphs can only go so far, so we celebrate a hollow win. Naturally, friends, kids, family, and, of course, pets, lift our spirits but only on a lower level—nothing like when we have someone to adore, and who cheers us on.

Love certainly enhances life and you can access it no matter how old, ugly, unhappy, nasty, and bitter you think you've turned out to be. I'm sure many of you know wicked people who wind up with the kindest partners you could ever imagine—and you wonder how on earth did those fiends ever get their rotten meat hooks into them? Once you learn how to access the vibration of love, it will transform everything you thought you knew about life. You become awake. Isolde underwent excruciating pain when it came to love, and will help any who ask her and she does the job *fast*, but only if you are open to receive her help. If your heart is frozen, nothing will change, and you may as well not even try. If this is the case, you need to thaw it out in little first—watch a couple romantic movies or read a book about lost love, and feel their pain.

I have been to Cornwall, a weird and wonderful region on the southwest English coast. It is steeped in history and tradition, and you are transported back in time upon arrival. A strange atmosphere permeates this mystical place and a fog descends early evening, as sadness ensconces this magical realm that defies all logical reason. At first I could not understand the vibration, and thought maybe pirates or Saxons had invaded and pillaged too much here—but the sorrow went much deeper than that. The tragic grief had to do with loss of true love, one that defies comprehension, which comes along just once in a lifetime.

Many years later I discovered that the crumbling castle I had stumbled upon was once home to a knight named Tristan. He had fallen deeply in love with a girl named Isolde, who had been promised to his beloved king. Upon collecting her as a royal duty, found they both fell in love along the journey. Legend says they had unknowingly been tricked into eating a love potion, making them fall for one another. This connection led to a tragic end for them, and the sorrow they endured seems to fan out into perpetuity. Arthurian legend was spun from their fatalistic encounter hundreds of years later, in 1470 AD, and the legend wasn't created out of thin air—something had transpired that left a footprint on that community, something that withstood the passage of time.

Two decades later I invoked Isolde and before going to bed asked her to please help me find true love. I went to sleep that night and woke to a brilliant silver light in my bedroom. It was so bright it lit up the whole space, and even with my eyelids closed I could not avoid it. I put the covers over my head, annoyed a spirit would keep me awake. I remember it stood there waiting, as if to say, "I'm here! I've come to help!" I closed my eyes, and the light was brilliant in my head; I opened them, and it was more blinding in the room. I put the blankets over my head and said, "Please, spirit, can we talk in the morning?" In answer, it disappeared in a long, startled vibration. The next morning I recalled the strange visitation, and was mortified to realize it must have been Isolde. I became instantly distressed, after I finally remembered calling her for help. I asked for her forgiveness, but she never came again. However, she created miracles in my world of love and fashioned a most righteous intercession. It was unbelievable what she did—and I am forever grateful. She radically changed my life, and she can do the same for yours. Just open your heart and ask.

Invocations to Isolde:

Dear Isolde, I ask you to please help me find true love, a soul mate to walk with me through life. I trust your guidance and love and believe in your intercession as I open my heart to move forward. Please allow me to forget blocks that have kept me alone as I move on to receiving this new phase of love. Thank you, Isolde, for bringing me the most treasured gift in the world. Blessings to you and all you bring toward me, Isolde. Thank you for changing my life.

Or

Dearest Isolde, I come to you with a broken heart and ask for you to please either help me repair the broken relationship, or help me move forward through the pain. I know at the end of the day you work in accordance with God's will, and I trust you will help pave the way. I only wish to love, as my time on this planet is short, and I pray you will help me in whatever direction best supports my soul. Thank you for helping me, Isolde; I am now positive again with love and feel the peace your kind heart has brought to my world. Thank you for bringing a healing to my romantic life, Isolde. I am forever grateful.

To see the mystical crumbling castle Isolde's
beloved Tristan lived in, go to YouTube and search:

Tintagel, King Arthur's Castle, Cornwall
All those memories; all that pain, so long ago.
You can almost see the horses running up the gate.

"Is your spirit real? I could be imagining you, just as easily as you stand here imagining me."

Ipos the Dark Angel, when we met in a dream.

CHAPTER 16

Ipos

A former dark angel he can be asked to assist in matters of the past, the future, for wisdom and courage and for making a difficult person leave you alone. He's like a lightning bolt in a bottle.

Commonly depicted with the body of an angelic being, head of a lion, tail of a hare, feet of a goose, and, in rare instances, even as a vulture. The ancients used these symbolic images to show how Ipos can cause you to fight, run, escape, or simply eat the enemy for lunch. We don't need to get medieval, but sometimes we have our back against the wall and playing paddy-cakes just won't do—and we need to make the aggressor stop before we break.

Ipos was once a powerful prince of Hell, with thirty-six legions of dark forces under his command. He was, according to ancient manuscripts, put under the spell of Solomon by a magical incantation, confined to a brass vessel sealed by mystical symbols, and now has to work for mankind. He has an edge and is the ideal spirit to invoke for a desperate situation. Is someone abusing you mentally, emotionally, or physically? Or is someone you love being mistreated? Ipos is your man. He's not to be used for amusement or to bring harm unnecessarily to others, but to protect you from getting bruised and beaten. If you invoke Ipos and try to use him for the wrong reason you will pay a very high price. I debated over inserting him into this anthology, but if used wisely he can actuate results in a dire situation. Where kindness, love, and understanding just won't do, and there's suffering incurred from an abusive perpetrator, send in Ipos and watch the fireworks begin.

When I was young and not sure who Ipos was, I went to sleep with him on the back burner of my mind. I found myself walking down a long train track, on a sunny day, in the countryside. The tracks led into a tunnel, and I kept walking to get through to the other side. The walls of the tunnel went from cement to a cave-like appearance and the end of the tunnel never came. I found myself in a long corridor lit by torches that led to a colossal, cavernous room with echoing sounds, in a cold, stark atmosphere. I turned to leave, and as I did so, I heard a man speak.

I looked around but saw no one- until I looked up. There suspended in midair from a giant swing made of ivy, was Ipos. He looked down and gazed at me with a concerned yet mocking stare. He looked like a very bad choir boy and as I tried to figure out if it was truly him, he tossed a fireball at me and announced in the dimly lit space, "I am Ipos. What can I do for you?" his quiet and calm demeanor spoke so much louder than his words, as his fireball sparked and hissed before disappearing at my feet.

I didn't know what to say and stuttered, wondering if I should even admit I wanted to see if he existed, if he was real, but to my horror he heard my thoughts.

"How can I not be real? What your spirit sees, hears and feels creates the reality that it sprung from. Even if I wasn't real your soul would create my existence, so what is the difference? I am a projection on the inside but once I get outside I become part of your reality- only because you see a result. You yourself created that wish but I am the source you tapped into to actuate its reality from. So I am real by default. Is your spirit real? I could be imagining you, just as easily as you stand here imagining me."

Now I really was muddled as he went on. "Energy is real, on that we can both agree. How it amalgamates itself depends upon the perceiver. Some may create me with blonde hair, some with blue—your projection creates who you perceive and how they appear. It's trite for people to disregard me when all I am is the essence of the energy you wish to invoke. I am from a source you need at the moment. If you go to get ice cream all you do is choose the flavor; spirits are the same." He paused, "I love ice cream."

I wasn't sure why he said that—except to let me know he could perceive just like I could, and in this altered world I was in with him, he was, in a sense, more real than I was at that moment in time.

He went on. "You are nothing more than a reflection; what becomes created from your interpretation of the energy all around you creates your total reality here. Your thoughts become a paradise or a perdition, since your projection becomes the reality of your essence, and your essence is all we care about here." I was processing his words when he interrupted my thoughts and said, "Do you like my swing?"

I looked at it as all the vines turned into snakes and kept dropping down on my head and all around me. Ipos laughed and said, "All you have to do is think, and they will become birds and fly away."

I wanted puppies, and they became hundreds of sweet little dogs that came up to greet me.

"Now do you see?" asked Ipos. "It's all a projection that turns into matter, and images give you a direction to do so. I am real; I exist; the question really is, do you? Are you real? From my world you are nothing more than a small pile of dust spun into a limited reality that has no idea it is blind. Pathetic." My charming host disappeared and I bent down to pet the puppies but they all turned into little lions that started nipping at my feet. I thought of them as flowers and saw the little monsters turn into lilies and in the distance I heard Ipos in a disembodied state say, "She's learning! Good little mortal!"

I collapsed back into reality and woke, enlightened, from my dream, thinking maybe spirits were all just a projection and it was really only us helping ourselves. In the dark, my computer suddenly turned itself on and searched the Internet until it found an apple pie dessert. Deep inside of my head I heard a voice say mischievously, "Goes good with ice cream!"

Think of Ipos like pepper spray. If you keep him in your back pocket, only use him in an emergency—otherwise, he could backfire and end up burning your eyes.

There's no prayer to Ipos—merely ask him to help you out and see him lobbing a fireball at your designated target. Thank Ipos in past tense. Imagine the problem melting away like ice cream in the sun. Give Ipos a slice of apple pie for thanks, and add a little plop of ice cream on top, too. He's got a lot of friends to back him up, so be warned: don't abuse his help! This angel's profile should come equipped with skull and cross bones. If he were a food he'd be a hot tamale.

"We're all one huge family, a great continuum.
Don't underestimate the power of the love created in
your homes and families. This love has an immense
potency; the power to influence other's lives in a
positive way."

Kuan Yin

CHAPTER 17

Kuan Yin

In Sanskrit, her name means "one who hears the words of the human world." She is the most beloved goddess and highly venerated deity in the Chinese pantheon. Known as Kannon in Japan, Avalokitesvara in India, Quan Am in Vietnam, and Spyan-rasgzigs or Bodhisattva Chenresi in Tibet. She bestows compassion, wisdom, and love to those who commune with her. If you talk about the Virgin Mary in the east, people think you mean Kuan Yin. She's especially prayed to by women; comforts the sick, senile, elderly, troubled, those frightened of a weather event, worry for any kind of animal; and the souls trapped in Purgatory can call on her to help release them. She is the Mother of the Universe, has a deep compassion for mankind, and is known as the Goddess of Mercy.

Kuan Yin was said to become enlightened while still here on Earth, making her a "Bodhisattva," and when her soul arrived at the Gates of Heaven, she was given entrance to Nirvana. Hearing the sorrows and lamentations of the people still on Earth, she refused entrance in order to come back down to the physical world and help her fellow man. Revered by Buddhists in eastern Asia, she possesses powers that make her one of their three greatest beings, renowned for commanding control over the animal kingdom as well as the mightiest forces of nature.

Buddhists believe just uttering her name invokes protection, and she has many temples all over China that passionately revere her name. She once resided in the Asian archipelago for nine years, on the tiny mountain island of Putuo Shan, off the coast of the Zhejiang Province. Basking in her legacy, by the year 1702 on that one island alone, there were over 400 monasteries with over 3,000 monks, though today there are only 140 monasteries and 1,000 monks. Still, to this day, thousands of pilgrims come there to pray to her, using rattles and fireworks to attract her attention.

She's had many incarnations, so can be depicted in many different ways. Interesting enough, she was a "he" in ancient days, until in the fourth century religious authorities decided he was actually a woman—but with an androgynous soul. Often she is seen barefoot sitting on a lotus flower, can have six to a thousand arms, a thousand eyes, and often rides a lion or a mythological animal called the Hou, which symbolizes her divine supremacy over the forces of nature.

Kuan Yin is a powerful energy to invoke for whatever lamentation or unhappiness surrounds your family life, animals, or desired weather event. A goddess of compassion, it is said no prayer to Kuan Yin goes unanswered. If you are having troubles with any situation, especially those that invoke emotional distress, call on her. She is the eastern version of the Virgin Mary, and works her miracles for anyone who asks for intercession. A powerful goddess, and people have been praying to her for thousands of years, so the collective unconscious energy she invokes reigns supreme, especially since her worshippers, in particular, are extremely devoted to her. If you have a daughter in the east, and people say she looks like Kuan Yin, it reigns as the ultimate compliment for beauty.

Novena to Kuan Yin:

I send this prayer to you dear Goddess Kuan Yin, and ask humbly for mercy and compassion, love and protection.

Please, kind goddess, hear my plea, and help me with (name your concern). Guide me throughout life and give me your support. Please help me to do the right thing to help myself as well as the others around me.

Please protect, bless and heal me. I do not wish to ask this of you selfishly, and many more here on Earth need your help, but perhaps do not know to call on you. I say this prayer to you for all who may need it, as well as me. I pray to you, blessed goddess, to help me (name your situation), and know that if it is accordance with God's will, I ask for your divine intercession.

Thank you, Kuan Yin, divine mother of compassion. I give you my eternal thanks for your blessing and protection! Thank you for helping me heal this hardship in my life. I am forever grateful to your kind dispensation, most kind and merciful Goddess. Namaste.

If you go to YouTube and look up **Kuan Yin**
you will find thousands of video streams,
and if you look up the island,
Putuo Shan, you will be impressed
by the splendor and glory of their devotion.

"Good can exist without evil, whereas evil cannot exist without good."

Thomas Aquinas (1225-1274 AD)

CHAPTER 18

St. Thomas Aquinas

Saint Thomas came from Sicily and was born in 1225 and died in 1274. He was a scholar of theology, ethics, metaphysics, politics, philosophy, and divinity. His nickname was "The Angelic Doctor", and his works have impacted modern philosophy even today, especially in the areas of natural law. He's considered one of the 33 Doctors of the Catholic Church, and is considered their greatest theologian and philosopher. A brilliant writer, St. Thomas can help you understand the unseen forces in your life- and how to activate the energy within. He can also teach you about angels and you can join him in a live, out-of-body class.

I awoke from an out-of-body trip, landing in a rather old fashioned classroom in Italy. I was the only student present as I sat down at an old desk that faced a chalkboard. It was a rather sparse classroom, but what stood out was this giant, old, brass skeleton key that hung above the chalkboard in midair. It was out of place, but all I remember thinking was, "I wish we still used those keys." At that moment a man entered through a door that suddenly appeared to the left of the room. It startled me, but then I thought, "I must be in an altered state," as the man in a brown Dominican priest's robe walked past me to the front of the room, and began to speak.

"I am Thomas Aquinas," he said. "I have something important to teach you." The calm man was intent that I listen to his words. My mind raced, trying to figure out who he was as he held an antique pointer at the chalkboard, which immediately turned into a giant hologram that enveloped us both into a charged gold energy field. There was an image of the outline of a human being floating horizontally, and upon its circumference were thousands of black keyholes.

St. Aquinas pointed to the keyholes and said, "This is how you go through life, with locked keyholes compiling your energy system. They can only be opened by the key of another being, one cannot do it themselves. Many of these keyholes are actually opened by strangers you randomly meet. Sometimes it takes two or three keys to open one keyhole, meaning you need to encounter more than one person to open certain locks." He lowered his voice. "That is why self-imposed exile kills the soul. That is why so many are unhappy. It becomes essential to become part of the flow of life by interacting with fellow beings."

I watched as other energy outlines came toward the silhouette of the human. Energy was exchanged, and a keyhole would suddenly turn into what I thought was a box, only to be told by Aquinas they were actually "windows and doors." "The keyholes turn into illumination that provides deeper access to your soul. These openings are essential if you wish to evolve faster in this body." He sighed and looked away. "So many go through their life in a complete locked state, causing them to have to repeat lessons through many worlds over and over again."

"Can these keyholes be unlocked by animals?" I know how deeply creatures impact us and wondered if something was happening we didn't understand.

Aquinas look pleased I had a question. "Yes, animals open doors, and often can help with opening ones that allow other windows and doors to open." He paused, then said, "There are some windows that are nearly impossible to open, but animals provide keys to open those, too." He turned and said under his breath something like, "If they only knew."

"Can plants or minerals open doors?" I was so happy to hear about the animals that at this point it didn't matter what he said.

"Minerals enhance but do not open; plants operate in a more clandestine operation that keeps energy flowing, but do know they are creatures that do exist." He paused. "There are so many in your galaxy. Beings and creatures you cannot fathom but interact with through your energy field all of the time. So much more goes on than anyone could realize." He stopped short as though no more information could be relayed, but then said, "Do you know who opens the most locks?"

"Back-stabbing friends?" I really wanted to pass this pop quiz.

"They are teachers indeed." Aquinas smiled. "But it's actually the vulnerable. We see who you really are around the helpless, the old, the infirm, the children, animals, and the poor. When you mistreat anything or anyone that is helpless it shall lock doors and windows that will never open again. Perhaps they will come in another lifetime, but they will be nearly impossible to open the second time around."

"I understand we need to open the locks to open windows and doors, but why are they important, sir?" I was so honored this man shared his brilliance with me that I wanted to be sure nothing went amiss.

"The doors have to do with your mind opening, while the windows are for direct evolvement of your soul. Both are necessary to ascend, *but if they stay locked for too many lifetimes, you cease to exist and are never seen again.*" He had a somber tone and look on his face as he went on. "If you cease to exist, you become matter, a dense, soulless substance that can no longer do harm. Matter creates all that you perceive—but what gives it *form* is God. God holds the final key."

I heard an old fashioned bell from far away, outside of the energy field we were in, as Aquinas kindly said, "I feel fortunate to teach you these concepts; too many are turning to matter now. We use the substance to bring new worlds into being but would rather have the souls. Heaven doesn't have as many entering in as it once did. There are many galaxies being built and colliding, and so all energy is used—but the perceivers are dwindling, and I hope you save a few. Helping those around you is God's way of helping you." He paused, seeming to want to say something more, but instead simply said, "You are always welcome here; but for now, class dismissed." He walked through the energy field as a group of angels walked through the "door" talking and laughing. One angel seemed to see me through the mist of the chalkboard and smiled as I waved back and faded to black.

Prayer to St. Thomas:
Grant me, St. Thomas, a mind to know God by helping those around me. I pray my locked aura finds the proper keys to set me free, so that I may better serve my fellow man and in so doing be your conduit for light and love to help the world of man ascend. I pray now in hope of finally thanking you and God for helping me through this troubling time (name of concern). Thank you, St. Thomas, for your powerful intercession and the potent

direction you gave me that helped me cope with (name issue) in my life. Amen.

For a beautiful video prayer to
St. Thomas Aquinas on YouTube, search:

**Eucharistic Prayer Of St Thomas Aquinas
("Pange Lingua Gloriosi Corporis Mysterium.")**

"I who love Him beheld Him with my own eyes which He made to see; and nearly touched Him with these my hands which He taught to reach forth."

**Mary Magdalene (thirty years later):
On the Resurrection of the Spirit**

CHAPTER 19

Mary Magdalene

A Love Affair to Remember

"And the companion of the savior was Mary Magdalene. Christ loved Mary more than all the disciples, and used to kiss her often on her mouth. The rest of the disciples were offended by it and expressed disapproval. They said to him, "Why do you love her more than all of us?" The Savior answered to them, "Why do I not love you like her?"

Gospel of Philip, dating from the second or third century, found in Nag Hammadi, southern Egypt, in 1945. A hoard of ancient papyrus books found in a sealed ceramic jar that never got public acclaim like the Dead Sea Scrolls, they show us a more intimate Jesus and the history of early Christianity.

Mary Magdalene was the absolute love of Jesus's life up until his final days of preaching. She was, sadly, the object of extreme jealousy and discontent among the disciples, who resented her for being taught so much more than they. They openly questioned Jesus for flaunting his attraction to her and were outraged a woman could be put on a higher level of confidence then a man. On meeting Jesus for the first time, Mary Magdalene said;

> He stood up and looked at me as the seasons might look down upon the field, and he smiled as he said, "All men love you for themselves. I love you for yourself." And then he walked away. But no other men ever walked the way he walked. Was it a breath born in my garden that moved to the east? Or was it a storm that would shake all things to their foundations? I knew not, but on that day the sunset of his eyes slew the dragon in me, and I became a woman. I became Miriam. Miriam of Midel.

According to Harvard divinatory scholar and theologian Karen King, Mary was considered the Apostle of the Apostles. She not only knew Jesus on a deeper level then the Apostles, but his innermost thoughts and his hopes and dreams as she testified on the speech and gestures of Jesus.

> I admired Him as a man rather than as a leader. He preached something beyond my liking, perhaps beyond my reason. And I would have no man preach to me. I was taken by His voice and His gestures, not by the substance of His speech. He charmed me but never convinced me; for He was too vague, too distant and obscure to reach my mind. I have known other men like Him. They are never constant nor are they consistent. It is with eloquence not with principles that they hold your ear and your passing thought, but never the core of your heart.

Mary was also present later when Jesus was whipped, beaten, ridiculed, had a crown of thorns impaled into his head, and was slashed by a giant gash into his side. She saw her beloved friend brutally beaten while being nailed to the cross by his hands and feet as he hung on the mount, where she helplessly knelt before him, weeping at his feet. The apostles—save for John—were like frightened children, and whirled away, scared the authorities would have them meet the same gruesome end. Mary Magdalene, his mother Mary, and his brother John, were there with him to his last, dying breath, supporting their beloved Jesus, who was no more than thirty-four years old when he was crucified.

The trauma Mary Magdalene endured was so much more than we have been taught. Mary had a harsh past (Jesus exorcised seven demons out of her), but Jesus kept her close, confiding in her and talking to her extensively about his dreams and visions. Mary said of him: "He was gentle, like a man mindful of his own strength. In my dreams I beheld the kings of the earth standing in awe in His presence."

Jesus found more awareness in Mary Magdalene than with the other apostles, who never quite understood the deeper meaning of his words. Mary Magdalene knew his soul and, watching him die, a part of her died, too.

It was also Mary Magdalene who went to his tomb to prepare his battered body for burial, but when she went inside found his corpse had disappeared. She assumed his body had been taken by the enemy, and in abundant grief ran out to the garden and collapsed in a fit of tears, the pain too hard to bear. Becoming hysterical, she couldn't stop gasping for breath as she drowned in tears at the horror of what must of gone on in her beloved's tomb. Why would they want his dead body? What further horrors could they inflict? She couldn't take the pain and cried inconsolably as someone came up behind her in the garden and asked her, "Why do you weep?"

"They have taken my Lord's body and I know not where it is." Mary assumed the gardener was speaking until he softly uttered, "Mary."

Mary now realized Jesus stood before her and screamed, "Master!" as she lurched forward to reach him to hold him in her arms.

He recoiled, saying, "Don't touch me, Mary!" as she realized she was gazing upon his arisen body and he must not be sullied by mortal hands. Jesus looked deeply into her eyes, and a love eternal fused into Mary's soul. At that moment, she understood that, though he stood before her, he was far beyond her reach. Separated by two worlds, the mundane and the divine, Mary respected the purity his soul commanded and forlornly gazed upon him.

Mary helped Jesus know love while here on the earthly plane, and, in so many ways, supported him so he could help us. We are much more indebted to her then we will ever know.

Jesus instructed her to go and tell the Apostles that he has risen from the dead. She desperately wanted to stay by his side, but obeyed and ran like wildfire to tell them the news. Mary Magdalene was the first person to see him arisen, but from this moment forward, she would never see her beloved again.

Constantly the apostles asked her questions about things Jesus told her, and when she honestly answered they would pounce, enraged that Jesus confided such important information to her. Over time they diminished her significance, and posterity was left out of the wisdom this blessed soul possessed. She was never a prostitute, not that it matters, or the woman who washed Jesus feet with her hair—all these inconsistencies were made by Pope Gregory the Great in his homily dated September 14, 591. He, like so many others, liked the thought that Mary was a sinner, repented, and was still loved by God. Perhaps Mary Magdalene would smile, knowing her alleged "tainted" reputation inadvertently helped lost souls feel good enough to come back to the church. Maybe this was her final sacrifice for her beloved Lord.

Mary was a great support to Jesus during the cataclysmic change that was going on at the time. The politically tumultuous climate they lived in was the setting in which it was terrifying to speak out about anything. This makes it clear why the Apostles lived every day frightened for their lives—it wasn't all loaves and fishes.

Mary teaches us to get past fear and do the right thing. She becomes a beacon for anyone who has ever lost their way and needed to get back on track. The pain she endured rings through the ages, but even through all that pain and suffering she still met her destiny and followed the last word of her Lord. She sets a shining example for us to follow our destiny, no matter what blocks our way, so that we have a faith that provides a lifeline to our soul.

Intercessory prayer to Mary Magdalene:

> Saint Mary Magdalene,
> who by conversion
> became the beloved of Jesus,
> thank you for your witness
> that Jesus forgives
> through the miracle of love.
>
> You, who already possess eternal happiness
> in His glorious presence,
> please intercede for me (name issue),
> so that someday
> I may share in the same everlasting joy."
>
> Amen.

For a fascinating and scholarly look at fragments of a lost gospel by the bewitching Mary Magdalene, indicating Mary Magdalene should have been the first pope, search for:

The Lost Gospel of Mary Magdalene

"Once again I say that with death Jesus conquered death, and rose from the grave a spirit and a power. And He walked in our solitude and visited the gardens of our passion. He lies not there in that cleft rock behind the stone."

Mary Magdalene (thirty years later):
On the Resurrection of the Spirit

"Excuse me while I kiss the sky."

Jimi Hendrix (November 27, 1942–September 18, 1970)

CHAPTER 20

Hendrix

"I wish they'd had electric guitars in cotton fields back in the good old days. A whole lot of things would've been straightened out."

When my friend Tom died, I had a horrible feeling he would not know he was dead, because he was alcoholic and did too many hallucinogenic drugs. He was a fallen angel with a brilliant mind and incredible charisma, and women would fall at his feet. He was kind and loving, always trying to make everyone feel better, though he lived his own life in torment and pain. He had lost everything that makes life worth living, including a Cambridge grad wife, a stellar scientific career, a beautiful home, friends, and every single cent he ever owned because it was spent on his addictive vices. Given everything from looks to brains, his succumbing to issues turned him into the quintessential All-American tragedy—left with no choice but to live under a bridge.

Being adept at leaving my body, I knew I had to reach him to make sure he was all right—or at least know he was dead, not on another bad trip. Tom had died driving a friend's motorcycle drunk on a lonely stretch of road, hitting a telephone pole with his chest, upon which he died instantly. When I finally found him in my astral projection he was covered in dirt. Upon seeing me he instantly became sparkly clean and said, "How did you find me out on this rad trip?"

I explained how he wasn't in a hallucination but had died in a motorcycle accident, and he needed to move on through this illusion toward the heavenly realm where souls were there to help him. He refused to believe he was dead, and in the end I had to show him his mother in order for him to really know the truth.

We had to go through these Swiss cheese-like tunnels that were complex labyrinths of time. I was still primarily of matter, so was a bit slower as he turned impatiently around and said, "Chop-chop!" We viewed his mother from above, crying in mourning with his photo near her side. His brothers were clinically cold doctors, and even they were distraught as we checked on them one by one.

Tom now realized the reality of his own death as a bright light appeared, with what seemed like his grandmother inside, signaling for him to come join her. He gazed gratefully into my eyes and faded away, but hollered out, "I'll see you later!" Assuming later was at death it saddened me—he was now finally gone—but I was glad I could let him know he had crossed to the other side.

A year later Tom appeared in a dream, and asked me to "step out" of my body, saying he had something "*unfrickenbelievable*" to show me. Other worlds, alien adventures, maybe an angel to talk to—my mind reeled at the prospects. It was awesome having angelic dead friends, and for once I was going to get to see something unbelievably cool! I remember thinking how lucky I was to be able to eject (from my body), although I found myself barely keeping up with Tom, as we suddenly found ourselves among an otherworldly mob. He had brought me someplace that was packed with an excited crowd, many of whom laughed and pointed at me. I had no idea what was going on and thought to myself "I wonder if I'm even allowed to be here." Tom was an expert at breaking the rules, and why should Heaven be any different than Earth? At this point I'd have wanted to kill Tom, if he wasn't already dead.

Tom had this weird glaze in his eyes and I wondered if maybe we were going to see the throne of God or some other hallowed scene. We stood surrounded by all kinds of people at what looked like a giant outdoor arena. "Tom," I bellowed through the throngs of spirits, "What's going on? Why are we here?" Tom assured me it was amazing, and as he spoke Jimi Hendrix took the stage. The crowd roared. I was so enraged I came all this way for a concert that I yelled at Tom, "I will never forgive you for dragging me to—," but at this moment I was in a soundproof chamber on the stage, that I can only equate to frosted ice that wasn't cold. The crowd cheered and howled as Hendrix did something to let the crowd know an un-dead was near.

He played a guitar and almost made it speak as he moved around my "cage," and sometimes I'd catch glimpses as he played the electric guitar gesturing toward me. I was forbidden from hearing the music, but I could feel the beat through my feet and became entranced by this virtuoso who played the guitar like nothing I had ever heard.

It was at this moment I realized that true genius was an energy sent from someplace above and it lifted hearts to be seen or heard, and the most unexpected source could bring home the divine. I honestly felt like much more than music was occurring, and it conducted a vibration from another place that healed our souls on some deep inner harmonic level. I couldn't hear the music, but I certainly could feel the vibration. In a way, I got a distilled version of the catharsis that occurred, simply by being exposed to the penetrating rhythm that makes your soul feel quenched. It made me aware that God found many sources to give the soul sustenance in everything, from a sound, to the scent of a rose, to a sunset we see, to a sweet dog we pet—and so many more secret codes we all have access to, if we are only open to receive.

I awoke back in my body after the concert ended, and even though I had hoped for some celestial vision, was granted access to a hidden source where true catharsis sprung. It became clear to me that we are all remote outposts from heaven and have a sending and receiving station hidden deep in our unconscious minds. This station can tune into whatever we home in on, and, by interfacing with the personality, a benefit is felt for all mankind. Finding the self and perfecting it thus becomes a humanitarian act. Hendrix came from abject poverty but still found his gift and in so doing made the whole world sing. He inspires us to allow the frequencies to flow, and use our disadvantages to push us further, to be the rock stars we were intended to be in our own life.

Invocation to Jimi Hendrix:

Your genius inspires me to let my spirit soar; your music fills the world and shows us all we can be whoever we want to be, as long as we let our spirit guide us. Jimi please help me to (mention your dream) so I, too, can help others find their place in the world. Thank you for your inspiration, god of rock!

On YouTube just search for **Jimi Hendrix**, and an endless succession of videos will pop up, each incredible and mesmeric.

"Your own soul is nourished when you are kind;
it is destroyed when you are cruel."

King Solomon (971-931 BC)

CHAPTER 21

Solomon

King Solomon **reigned supreme** for over forty years as the king of the United Kingdom of Israel and Judah 971–931 BC. Solomon was a righteous king and known throughout the ancient world as being one of the wisest men to have ever lived. He had many mystical instruments, and, according to Arabic legend, it was he who put the genie in the bottle.

Most of us have never had anyone to count on or solve problems for us, and have had to make decisions for ourselves. Many of the tiniest worries turn into lifelong issues if we don't make the right choice in the foothills of concerns. Praying helps us to get guidance, but to really turbocharge the answer, ask Solomon for advice. It will startle you that the right answer for your decision comes in a clear flash of illumination; this occurs because Solomon sends wisdom almost instantaneously, instead of going through the muck and the mire of intellect, which often gets in the way. A really good habit to get into when you need to make a decision is say to yourself, "Solomon, what would you do?" and be prepared for an immediate response. It's not that Solomon will appear in velvet robes with cocktails and pomegranates (which he believed were aphrodisiacs), but he will illuminate an answer that is far outside the (jeweled) box.

According to rabbinical literature, before becoming king, Solomon modestly asked God to please just grant him wisdom, so that he could reign over his kingdom fairly and justly:

> And the king went to Gibeon to sacrifice there; for that was the great high place: a thousand burnt offerings did Solomon offer upon that altar. In Gibeon the LORD appeared to Solomon in a dream by night: and God said, Ask what I shall give thee. And Solomon said, Thou hast shown unto thy servant David my father great mercy, according as he walked before thee in truth, and in righteousness, and in uprightness of heart with thee; and thou hast kept for him this great kindness, that thou hast given him a son to sit on his throne, as it is this day. And now, O LORD my God, thou hast made thy servant king instead of David my father: and I am but a little child: I know not how to go out or come in. And thy servant is in the midst of thy people whom thou hast chosen, a great people that cannot be numbered nor counted for multitude. Give therefore thy servant an understanding heart to judge thy people that I may discern between good and bad: for who is able to judge this thy so great a people? (1 Kings 3:4-9)

God answered back to Solomon's humble request: "Since you have asked for this and not for long life or wealth for yourself, nor have asked for the death of your enemies but for discernment in administering justice, I will do what you have asked..." (1 Kings 3:11-12)

The Hebrew Bible also states that: "The whole world sought audience with Solomon to hear the wisdom God had put in his heart." (1 Kings 10:24)

Perhaps the most famous story of Solomon's wisdom is of the two women, each claiming a baby was hers, who were brought to the throne of Solomon, both with convincing arguments. Solomon had a guard raise his sword because, Solomon decided, both mothers should win. As the guard got ready to chop the baby "down the middle," one of the women dropped to her knees and begged Solomon to give the baby to the other woman. Solomon gave the baby to the woman who was willing to lose the child in order to let it live. It was obvious she loved the baby most. There's another, lesser-known story that underscores his ability to discern, but this one takes place with a two-headed man.

A father with two heads married a woman with one and they, depending how you look at it, had six and a half kids. The father died and his inheritance was about to be split up between the children, but one of those children also had two heads, just like his double-headed daddy. The double-headers were outraged because they felt they should have two inheritances, instead of the one to split between them. Solomon pondered this odd enigma and decided they should only get one inheritance, because they only had one body to sustain the two heads, and if it died, both heads would roll.

During Solomon's forty-year reign, he wrote three books:

- The Book of Wisdom—a collection of fables and wisdom of life.
- Ecclesiastes—a book of contemplation and self-reflection.

- The Song of Solomon—a chronicle of erotic love (there are contrasting opinions that the subject could be women or God).

Solomon was reported to have had an unprecedentedly glorious realm, evidenced by his collection of great material prosperity, found in rebuilt cities, temples, sea ports, commercial depots, and military outposts. He amassed 1,400 chariots and 12,000 horsemen; he had 700 wives and 300 concubines (all of whom desperately loved him); and gained an epic splendor of wealth—in a single year alone he collected 39,960 pounds of gold. These facts can be backed-up by phenomenal, gigantic, and intact archeological relics found in six major cities Solomon either strengthened or rebuilt. He was a wondrous man, who was also said to have some serious mystical powers, which included sublime instruments with which to procure even more advancements and success. A magical key, mechanical throne, and his magical table were low on the totem pole of tools Solomon possessed. The "Seal of Solomon" was his prized magical ring, given to him by God, which gave him power over demons. Solomon enslaved several hundred legions of demons, including their demon king. Today, we know the formidable icon that was stamped upon his ring as the Star of David.

The earliest followers of the Kabbalah spoke extensively of Solomon sailing through the air on a throne made of light, or a magic carpet, which could travel so fast, it was reported it could get from Damascus to Medina within one day. This magical flight machine not only brought him to the gates of heaven, but also to the dark mountains which held the fallen angels. Uzza and Azzazel were two of the fallen angels that were chained-up there, and Solomon, using the magic ring, would compel them to tell him every single mystery he wished to know. Solomon also was said to force his enslaved demons to take his friends on day trips to hell. Solomon was like a hip-hop mogul with money, friends, chariots, girls, and a seriously wild ride, but his greatest legend of all time was the genie in a bottle.

A well-known legend was in the story of *One Thousand and One Nights*, where Solomon lost his patience with a genie. This genie upset Solomon so much, he forced the little rascal into a bottle and threw it out to sea. Solomon had locked the bottle with his magic seal so that sneaky genie could never escape. It wasn't until many centuries later that the genie was released from his prison by a passing fisherman.

Perhaps this legend has more to do with Solomon's rebuttal of his own carnal temptations, as opposed to any living, breathing creature that can make all dreams come true. There's also a reoccurring theme throughout many ancient texts that present the principal with an excessive amount of temptation they must rebuke in order to receive the blessings of God.

Solomon slid a bit from grace by becoming drunk with success and power, and in the end God divided his kingdom apart after his son took the crown. What we need to focus on, however, is the brilliant soul Solomon commanded that helped all those who came into contact with him. A brilliant thinker and wise sage, Solomon shows us the world is our oyster, if we will only choose to do good and leave our insecurities behind. It isn't the devil we need to watch out for; we need to watch out for the one who always gets in our way—ourselves.

When you are unsure of what to do, invoke Solomon's wisdom, then get out of the way of yourself and see the answers tumble down into awareness—but only when you are open to receive.

Invocation to Solomon:

Please show me the correct solution Solomon; I am open to receive. Thank you, Solomon, for helping me with (name situation). I am grateful for your wisdom and sage advice.

There is an interesting one minute clip on the aerial view of King Solomon's Temple, based on ancient ruins from 70 AD. Go to YouTube and search for:

Solomon's Temple - 3D Aerial Tour.

"*The holy Heaven yearns to wound the Earth,
and yearning layeth hold the earth to join in
wedlock; the rain, fallen from the amorous heaven,
impregnates the earth, and it bringeth forth for
mankind the food of flocks and herds and Demeter's
gifts; and from that moist marriage-rite the woods
put on their bloom. Of all these things I Aphrodite,
goddess of procreation, am the cause.*"

Aeschylus, Fragment 25 Danaides
(from Athenaeus, Deipnosophists xiii. 73. 600B)
(trans. Smyth) (Greek tragedy C5th BC)

CHAPTER 22

Aphrodite

Ancient Greek **Goddess** of love, procreation, sexual rapture and dazzling beauty. Ancients believed she was born from sea foam, and thus inspired the beautiful painting by Botticelli, stepping out of a giant clam shell, standing there nude in full glory.

It was said that Zeus worried that because Aphrodite was so drop dead gorgeous, the gods would fight over her hand for marriage. So he married her off to the god of smiths, Hephaestus. Zeus thought Hephaestus would treat her well and was the safest of all the gods. Hephaestus was overjoyed to have such a stunning wife and wanted to do something so spectacular for her, she would love him forever. Being a smith, he made her gorgeous jewels, but eventually feared even this was not enough. So Hephaestus used all his expertise to create a precious, golden girdle with magical powers woven into the delicate filigree fibers.

Upon wearing the girdle, however, Hephaestus's plan backfired, as Aphrodite became even more seductive to mortals as well as gods—and she loved every moment of it. This attention made her even more disgusted by the fact she was married to an old, dirty goat. Hephaestus was devastated as she seduced one young handsome god after another. In the end, she ran off with Adonis, and she even dumped him for the god Anchises, to whom she bore another son.

The Three Graces who always surrounded Aphrodite were Aglia (beauty), Euphrosyne (happiness), and Thalia (good cheer). These were daughters of Zeus and a nymph. They were considered the essence of beauty and grace, and were the energy that helped Aphrodite seduce so many lovers, inspiring artists and bringing pleasure to men. They were all always nude. They had outrageous parties, and were worshipped in various festivals called the Aphrodisiac, especially in Athens and Corinth. Though today one might consider her priestesses prostitutes, they were merely using the method of sex to worship the gods. In Roman mythology, Aphrodite was known as the goddess Venus, the conductor of love and beauty.

In Greek mythology, Pygmalion was a sculptor who could not find love. The women of his village thought it wrong he was still single, so invoked Aphrodite to make him pick a wife. Poor Pygmalion had no interest in the women of his village, and when Aphrodite appeared to tell him to pick one or else she would, he panicked. He asked Aphrodite if he could first sculpt a statue of her before he made his choice. Flattered, Aphrodite accepted. Pygmalion formed the statue while becoming nauseated that when it was done, he would be forced to marry one of the women of his town. He finished the statue but desperately needing more time from having to choose a hideous wife, started to turn his beautiful creation into somebody else, even naming it "Galatea." When Aphrodite returned, she was ready to help him choose, not to mention sick of waiting for him to stop fumbling with that ridiculous statue that bore no resemblance to her whatsoever. She was going to make a husband of this artist if that was the last thing she did.

The desperate sculptor had, somewhere along chiseling the stone statue, fallen deeply in love with his creation. Aphrodite, however, absolutely refused to let him marry a stone. Pygmalion wrapped his arms around the life-sized statue and begged Aphrodite to please make Galatea come to life. Aphrodite refused; there were plenty of desperate girls who wanted to be with the handsome sculptor.

Pygmalion cried out in horror, "If you cannot make Galatea alive, then *turn me into stone so I may be by her side!*" Aphrodite was so deeply touched by his deep devotion she turned the statue into a live, breathing lady. Pygmalion fell so madly in love with her they soon married and lived happily ever after.

Galatea

Moral of the story? You can't make someone love you, regardless of your beauty and your charm. Also, if somebody does love you, let them in and maybe it will bring you back to life. Aphrodite, with all her charm, beauty and powers could not force the sculptor to change his heart, and even though she thought a stone statue was beneath him and there were many women waiting, the heart knows what it truly loves and no one or nothing can change it.

Invocation to Aphrodite:

"Beautiful Aphrodite, I beseech your help and ask you to (find, heal, bring back love, make me more attractive to <name person>, or enhance my beauty). I am grateful for all your support and thank you, Aphrodite, with all and every part of my heart. Thank you for making it sing again, thank you for making me effervescent with beauty. I am eternally grateful, sweet goddess."

A tranquil and enchanting short clip on
YouTube to watch while invoking
Aphrodite can be found by searching for:

Second Life. The Temple of Aphrodite

"Put your faith in God to let me heal you of your cancer."

From the mind of Saint Peregrine (1260-1345)

CHAPTER 23

Saint Peregrine

Born in Forli, Italy (1260–1345), he is known throughout Europe as the patron saint of cancer, and is also invoked for problems with legs and bad rashes. He bestowed thousands of public miracles and staggered the scientific community of his time.

Many of the saints start out full of piss and vinegar, as the saying goes, yet wind up leading quite virtuous lives. It's as though unless they learn how to harness their exceptional talents, they spin out of control and drive everyone around them insane. Peregrine was no exception. Born into an extremely wealthy family (like many of them are), he became very active politically and even joined an anti-papal society that disturbed the peace and tranquility of Italy. He was, for want of a better word, a rapscallion.

St. Philip, also known as the Apostle of Rome, had come to preach peace to the heathen town of Forli, but St. Peregrine heckled and publically humiliated him, before leading a troop of thugs to beat him up with stones and clubs. To end the cruel spectacle, St. Peregrine punched him in the nose and knocked poor St. Philip out cold.

A gentle soul, St. Philip realized there was not going to be any welcome party forthcoming and calmly dusted himself off and left to get back home to Rome. St. Peregrine made a mockery of St. Philip, and even knocked him out by punching him in the nose, but then had a strange transformation of conscience and chased him three miles up the road to beg for his forgiveness. Saint Philip consoled the penitent young man and instructed him to pray to the Holy Mother Mary.

Peregrine prayed as instructed, but to his amazement had a vision of the Holy Mother, who told him to go to Sienna and said, "There you will find my servants." Peregrine went on the journey, hoping to find St. Philip. There his battered buddy was not to be found, but instead he encountered the Servants of Mary, also known as the Servites. It was here he began a penance that went on for quite some time. He decided to only stand unless sitting was necessary, in honor of God, and in so doing didn't sit for the next thirty years. He also would not speak unless it had to do with God, and would only sleep on the ground with a rock instead of a pillow. His austere life was a far cry from the wealth and privilege he was raised in, where even his parents were a bit debauched. Peregrine committed to and lived this austere life in total for over sixty-two years.

This somber saint got a severe cancer of the foot that gave off such a foul stench people ran from him on the street. He was going to have it amputated, but the night before his operation he began to pray intensely. Peregrine had a vision that would shock the scientific community of his time. He saw Jesus on the crucifix, where he stretched out his hand to cure the diseased foot. The next morning Peregrine awoke to a perfectly healthy foot, with no cancer and no sign of disease.

His startling miracle inspired others to come to him for aid, and St. Peregrine publically performed shocking numbers of miracles—as well as private ones—by whispering prayers in Jesus's name into the ear of the recipient. Peregrine was well-known for often multiplying bread for the poor. Being a former bad boy, Peregrine also accomplished a more amusing feat, when he rounded up Italy's worst forty outlaws and got them to repent and help the victims they had bamboozled.

You can pray to St. Peregrine for any miracle, but he's the patron saint for cancer.

Prayer to St. Peregrine for people with cancer:

O great St. Peregrine, you have been called "The Mighty," "The Wonder-Worker," because of the numerous miracles which you have obtained from God for those who have had recourse to you.

For so many years you bore in your own flesh this cancerous disease that destroys the very fiber of our being, and you had recourse to the source of all grace when the power of man could do no more. You were favored with the vision of Jesus coming down from His Cross to heal your affliction. Ask of God and Our Lady, the cure of the sick whom we entrust to you.

(Pause here and silently recall the names of the sick for whom you are praying.)

Aided in this way by your powerful intercession, we shall sing to God, now and for all eternity, a song of gratitude for His great goodness and mercy.
Amen.

If you want to hear me speak of Saint Peregrine firsthand
and do a meditation to actually go and meet him,
go to YouTube and search for:

Cancer Cure with Saint Peregrine
(can also be used for any other worry)

Hippocrates is someone you may also want to read about—I've inserted a recipe here for a five-thousand-year-old soup concotion that cures cancer and heals other disease.

"*Prayer indeed is good, but while calling on the gods, a man should himself lend a hand.*"

Hippocrates (460-370 BC)

CHAPTER 24

Hippocrates

Hippocrates (460-370 BC) lived in ancient Greece and was the father of modern medicine. He firmly believed diet directly impacted health, and came up with this famous soup to combat disease, digestive disorders, and raise the immune system by detoxifying the liver, a soup that fights all types of acute and chronic diseases. Now, the most sophisticated physicians who lead the way in science tell people to go home and eat Hippocrates Soup while taking their medicine!

Often, when I was young, I had strange visions. Sometimes I thought it was God or an angel or saint who told me about "divine medicine." Everything seemed to operate through *vibrations*, and they taught me how the *essence* often had more impact than what presided in the real world. Most of the time I never really understood—as was the case here—until I got much older and was able to turn their words into wisdom.

When I was about nine years old, a man in a long brown robe came to teach me in a dream. He showed me a flower I'd never seen before that seemed to glow and spin, telling me it was called a lotus flower. Growing up in the Midwest, I'd never seen such a flower. Then he showed me close-ups of its root, explaining that it had some kind of medical power to cure cancer. I told the message to many grownups, who just shook their heads and patted me on the back, asking me in whispers if I'd eaten any funny mushrooms.

New studies are now coming out that have scientific documentation that the lotus root does indeed transmit curative powers, one of which, of course, is anti-cancer. He concocted a truly mouthwatering soup from the depths of deep reflection, science, and ancient wisdom. He wanted to change the way you treat your body and make you aware that certain phytochemical amalgamations (that is, certain plant-based foods put together) create a symbiosis that is so sophisticated we cannot understand it, but we know it helps the system reach a state of homeostasis, making it dramatically shrink tumors, and sometimes causing the body to go into a complete state of remission—if not cured completely.

Visualize pure white snow covering black rocks, and as you do, breathe in through the bottom of your feet. You may feel a slight pulsing or tingle—this is *earth energy* and it raises the immune system (among other things). Do this to remove any growths, tumors, cysts, lumps—anything you want *out* of your body.

I can lead you through this on YouTube, just search for:

How to Access Earth Energy for Money, Love and the Immune System

CHAPTER 25

Hippocrates Soup

(as it appears in Angelic Healing Soups *(hope in* **a pot)** **by Angel Cusick)**

A 2,500 year old **recipe dispense**d by leading physicians
even today to detoxify kidneys and put extra zing
in your wings. Fights all types of acute and chronic
diseases, aids in digestion, cleanses the liver, and has even
been known to heal halos.

Its ingredients and profound propensities include: celery
(contains eight different anticancer compounds, combats high
blood pressure, and is a mild diuretic), parsley root (anticancer compound, antioxidant, and mild diuretic), leeks (loaded
with vitamin C), tomatoes (anticancer, potent antioxidant),
onions (anti-inflammatory, profound antioxidant, antiviral,
anticancer; thins blood; lowers cholesterol; raises good cholesterol; wards off blood clots; fights asthma, chronic bronchitis,
hay fever, diabetes, atherosclerosis, and infections), potatoes
(anti-cancer, helps prevent high blood pressure because it's
loaded with potassium), garlic (a wonder drug that does everything you can possibly think of), moonbeams and filtered
waterfalls from secret places…(we can't disclose the wherea-
bouts…otherwise we'd have to take you down).

1 celery root (can be found in health food or Asian shops).
1/2 bunch parsley, finely chopped and set aside to finish soup (about 1 cup)
1 medium parsnip
2 small leeks
2 28-oz. cans diced tomatoes (save 1 1/2 cup for finishing the soup)
2 medium yellow onions
4 medium golden potatoes (about a pound)
3 cloves garlic
Filtered water to cover veggies
2 tsp. salt

Peel celery root, wash and scrub potatoes and parsnip, then coarsely dice in large chunks; peel and smash garlic cloves; peels and coarsely dice yellow onion; cut leeks to the green part and cut in half, and clean really well under running water before coarsely chopping. Cover with water, add cans of diced tomatoes (don't drain; also, set aside 1 1/2 cup diced tomatoes to add to soup after the soup is pureed) and simmer until tender, about two hours. Puree with a soup wand, then add the finely chopped parsley and reserved diced tomatoes. Makes approx. 24 cups

When you eat the soup, see tiny soldiers beating the crap out of aliens. Give thanks to Hippocrates who must have spent a lot of time in the cave writing this down.

*If you wish to find more soup recipes, go to Amazon.com, CreateSpace.com and other book outlets and search for:

*Angelic Healing Soups**

"Whatever you give away at death for the Lord's sake you give because you cannot take it with you. Give now to the true Savior, while you are healthy, whatever you intended to give away at your death."

Saint Lucy instructing her mother to distribute all her inherited jewels and great wealth to the poor.

CHAPTER 26

Santa Lucia

Saint Lucy, also known as Santa Lucia, lived between the years of 283 and 304. Her name comes from Latin "lux" which means light, clear, radiant and understandable. She is the patron saint of the beast, blind, people with eye issues, and those who need to "see the light" in a difficult situation. She died a martyr at the tender age of twenty-one. Her body lies incorrupt over 1,700 years later.

Born in Sicily to an extremely wealthy family, Lucia actually lived alone with her mother, her father dying when she was quite young. The mother suffered from dysentery for many years, but had heard that the passed-over St. Agatha performed miraculous intercessions from her grave. The two went to her graveside and prayed all night, and when Lucia finally fell asleep at the grave, St. Agatha appeared to her in a vision. Agatha told her, "Soon you shall be the glory of Syracuse, as I am of Catania." The next morning the mother was healed and no longer needed her daughter to care for her. Lucia was relieved since, due to exhaustion, she and her mother had fallen asleep at the graveside and were unable to stay up the whole night to pray.

Desperately wanting grandchildren, the Italian mother now arranged for Lucia to marry a wealthy nobleman, but upon finding he was a pagan Lucia refused. She really wanted the money and jewels that were to be her dowry, to be distributed to the alms for the poor. Lucia wanted only to help her fellow man and had no interest whatsoever in her vast inheritance, marriage, or children.

A gossiping nurse told the rejected nobleman that she had heard Lucia found a better suitor with more money and better looks than anyone had ever seen. The bridegroom became enraged, and in retaliation reported her Christian beliefs to the magistrate. This action was the equivalence of a death sentence, since it was the very beginning of the Diocletian Persecution (meaning the Great Persecution), which was the last and most horrifically bloody persecution of Christians ever known in the Roman empire, lasting from 303–313.

In court, the magistrate felt sorry for Lucia, since she was so young and kind and he only asked her to burn a sacrifice to the Emperor's image. Lucy brazenly replied "All I have to offer him is myself; let him do his own offerings." The court was outraged at her offensive behavior, and the magistrate then sentenced the virgin to be defiled in a brothel. Lucy had an answer for that, too.

No one's body is polluted so as to endanger the soul if it has not pleased the mind. If you were to lift my hand to your idol and so make me offer against my will, I would still be guiltless in the sight of the true God, who judges according to the will and knows all things. If now, against my will, you cause me to be polluted, a twofold purity will be gloriously imputed to me. You cannot bend my will to your purpose; whatever you do to my body that cannot happen to me.

The court broke into pandemonium as guards rushed forth to take her away, but when they surrounded her something miraculous happened—they could not move her. Lucia announced that the "Holy Spirit" was making her strong. The livid guards said she was as stiff and heavy as a mountain, so in desperation hitched her (from the courtroom) to a team of oxen, but even that could do nothing to budge her. One of the soldiers, frustrated he couldn't get the frail girl to move, impaled a dagger straight through her throat—but Lucia started talking like nothing had happened and prophesied against the brutal men. The soldiers thought to finally silence her they would burn her to death, so they piled wood around her feet and set flames afire—but she would not burn. The stakes were now heavily raised.

The guards proceeded to go into a frenzy, tearing off her clothes and cutting off her breasts. When she came through that still alive and showing no sign of pain, the soldiers grabbed a fork and viciously gouged out her eyes. Lucy made a calm response after the degradation and incomprehensible torture: "Now let me live to God."

History now becomes murky because of shame involved in the incident, but what took place is confirmed by many sources. It's widely held that the soldiers finally killed her by slicing her into a million pieces so she would never be heard of again—or so the authorities thought.

Santa Lucia became such an inspiration to the Christian movement she was one of the seven women aside from the Blessed Virgin Mary commemorated by name in the Canon of the Mass, proclaiming Santa Lucia a true Christian martyr. Lucia was painted many times over, showing her holding her eyes on a golden platter with her vision restored by God.

Even to this day many churches commemorate her by making sweet Lucy their namesake. In Omaha, Nebraska, they hold the Santa Lucia Festival, founded in 1925 by Italian immigrants, every summer. A statue of St. Lucy is paraded through the downtown streets, along with a relic from the actual body of St. Lucy. You may want to attend this if you suffer from breast or eye worries, and try to touch the relic.

Invocation to Santa Lucia:

Saint Lucy, you did not hide your light under a basket, but let it shine for the whole world, for all the centuries to see. We may not suffer torture in our lives the way you did, but we are still called to let light illumine our daily lives. Please help us to have the courage to bring our faith into our work, our recreation, our relationships, our conversation—every corner of our day. Saint Lucy, please intercede on my behalf to (name concern) with your light and brave beliefs. Thank you, Saint Lucy, for healing my desperate plea with your kind intercession. I am forever grateful. Amen.

"In the name of the unity of the tabernacle of the Lord, and the dwelling of the Lord, it is secret and hidden. Blessed is the name of the glory of the kingdom forever. See it restore the glory of life everlasting. Endure therein and know every science of secret and hidden things."

The Book of the Angel Raziel
Written by the Archangel Raziel

CHAPTER 27

Archangel Raziel

His name means "The Keeper of Secrets of the Lord." Invoke Raziel when you need wisdom, manifestation, clarity from hidden truths, direction, to understand quantum physics, sacred geometry, wish to hear God's guidance more clearly, or to enhance clairvoyant skills.

Raziel was said to sit by the throne of God, and was privy to sacred secrets not one of the other angels knew anything about. The angel of sacred mysteries, he reveals holy secrets only when God gives him the green light. Ancients, including Solomon, believed his book imparted great wisdom to the reader, and illumination was bestowed when one pondered divine thought. *The Book of the Angel Raziel* analyzes divine secrets about both celestial and earthly knowledge, where God's secret insights into the universal mechanics of being are revealed.

Raziel begins the book by saying, "Blessed are the wise by the mysteries coming from the wisdom." Raziel inferred that creative energy begins with thoughts in the spiritual realm that lead to words, actions, and manifestation in the physical realm.

Raziel illuminates the components of the soul and places them in five different portions of being:

1. The breath of life
2. The soul itself
3. The mind
4. The life or vitality of the spirit (this is code for destiny)
5. Uniqueness of the soul and how it in turn interfaces with the unity of others

The Angel also described the seven degrees of hell, which Hebrew mythology replicated in its description:

1. Hell
2. The Gates of Hell
3. The Shadow of Death
4. The Pit of Destruction
5. The Clay of Death (reminds me of what Thomas Aquinas warned)
6. The Perdition (punishment)
7. Triple Hell (you might as well give up at this point)

It profoundly describes being human and what the soul has to gain or win through its voyage hidden from detection in the guise of skin and bones. The book also makes clear that only pure souls will be able to understand its wisdom and profit from its teachings. Profane and irreverent people will encounter a block while reading it, and not be able to process its deeper meaning. The reader must also possess some form of psychic acumen and invoke insight from the author, Raziel.

In ancient manuscripts, it has been said that the book first made its illustrious appearance back in the Garden of Eden, and who we believe to be Adam and Eve actually started out as Adam and Lilith. Lilith was not of human origin and was beyond disgusted having to be with a "dirt creature." In horror, she ran away from Adam, and, for many thousands of years, ancients lived in fear of her retribution. Worried she would start killing off their babies, they kept certain cryptograms for protection hung upon the infant's crib to keep Lilith from killing them while they slept, part of a bigger plot she hatched to snuff the human race.

Adam lamented being so alone on the Earth, so God created a cohort out of Adam's rib, to make sure no one pulled rank on Adam this time round. Adam (who always seemed unstable to me), was still overwhelmed by this new world, so God told the angel Raziel to write the mechanics of how the universe worked in a book that would detail how it functioned. It is said when Raziel gave the book to Adam and he began to read it, all the angels stood behind his back and read the text over his shoulders, because it was filled with so many divine secrets none of them knew.

In the myth of "The Fall from Grace," Eve, tempted by the serpent, got Adam to eat the fruit from the forbidden tree. It was said there were thousands of trees to choose from, but Eve decided to take a bite out of the one apple God absolutely forbade. When God came to confront them for the disobedience, they were suddenly ashamed they had no clothes on and God knew their innocence was lost. Brats!

God was pretty disappointed that his beloved firstborns broke the rules, and we all know what happened next—or do we? God instructed Raziel to take the book back from Adam and let them scratch out a meager existence without his wise counsel. Raziel took the tome back and all hell broke loose. Adam literally had a nervous breakdown, which he was headed to for a long time. The man had so many harsh lessons and he was so naïve, that his soul just gave up trying and he fell into sorrow and pain.

In defiance, Adam stood in the river up to his head and threatened to commit suicide if God didn't give back the book. I can only imagine what Eve went through; she probably wished she'd just stayed on as a rib. In the end, God capitulated and gave the book back. Adam came out of the water and life went on, though it's sad to think the first human being wanted to become brown bread (that's Cockney rhyming slang for "dead").

It is said Enoch (only human to turn angelic, into Archangel Metatron), Noah and Solomon gleamed all their wisdom from this book. When you read ancient texts, people rave about Solomon and what extraordinary wisdom he possessed. Solomon credits it all to *The Book of the Angel Raziel.* The book has been rumored to have been penned by a Jewish scholar in the middle ages, by a man named Eleazar of Worms or Isaac the Blind. If this were the case, how could Solomon of used it in ancient day so extensively? The original book, it is widely believed, was kept in a house of treasures, and while it was missing people tried to replicate its message. You can buy the book today—but be warned it may not make sense. Like the Egyptian scrolls that held three levels of meaning depending upon one's education in the ancient mystery school studies, this book requires a psychic dimension in the reader. I have to say, though, you may like having the energy of the book around—it might make you feel lucky. I suggest you put it under your bed, mattress, or pillow, allowing your unconscious to get bathed in his divine, energetic light.

Raziel emphasizes the importance of love and says

It is decreed, as it is written, Abraham was beloved. God spoke to him to lead his son. It is written, you know to revere God. You know of love. Know it is decreed, man is happy not to journey by counsel of wickedness. It is written herein, man is happy to revere the Lord. Show reverence to the heavens all the day. Regard love in the heart. The reverence of the heavens is in the heart at all times, reverence of the purity of the Lord. Those giving reverence are loved by the Lord. There is much value in living in purity. Bathed in the glory of the light of God. Go from darkness into light, divided from those led astray. As the light shines down upon the sea, that is the reverence of God who spoke to Abraham. From love, understanding was created by the love and reverence. A thousand generations come after from the love.

In accordance with Raziel's direction, ask him to help you, especially if you need to make a decision on something that isn't clear. Know that he's an archangel, not your guardian variety escort, and invoke him when you need clarity or have issues that require deeper understanding. He is a benevolent angel and brings wisdom with sudden waves of elucidation—don't expect him to appear in all his glory with wings and Raphael's trumpet. He's much more subtle than that.

Invocation to Raziel:

Dearest Archangel Raziel, I come to you to ask for your divine illumination and direction to show me the way in this confusing subject (name issue). I honor your wisdom and forever am grateful for your guidance in this life. Thank you, Archangel Raziel, for bringing such celestial insight into my life. It has made all the difference and helped me. Amen.

To hear Angels accidentally caught on tape singing—this is truly spectacular—go to YouTube and search:

Angels Singing Recorded!

There's also another video of the witnesses who were there that night. This is a growing phenomenon—maybe they are trying to get through to us as we enter difficult times. I sense they want us to believe in them again, so we are also able to accept the support they wish to accord.

"*I believe in everything until it's disproved. So I believe in fairies, the myths, dragons. It all exists, even if it's in your mind. Who's to say that dreams and nightmares aren't as real as the here and now?*"

John Lennon (1940–1980)

CHAPTER 28

Morgan le Fey, Fairy Queen

Her legend originated in ancient Welsh literature that later inspired the sorceress in Arthurian Legend. She is a formidable archetype to invoke from the fairy kingdom, which, once unraveled, presents a sprite that invokes intense protection for the natural world. Use Morgan le Fey (means "fairy" in French) to support whatever efforts you try to make in the plant world, such as growing flowers, a garden, or even helping a dying tree or a house plant.

The Fairy Kingdom
Q. Can you describe the shining beings?
A. It is very difficult to give any intelligible description of them. The first time I saw them with great vividness, I was lying on a hillside alone in the West of Ireland in County Sligo. I had been listening to music in the air, and to what seemed to be the sound of bells, and was trying to understand these aerial clashings in which wind seemed to break upon wind in an ever changing musical silvery sound. Then

the space before me grew luminous, and I began to see one
beautiful being after another.
Walter Evans-Wertz
The Fairy Faith in Celtic Countries
London Oxford University Press 1911

These rather potent vibrations' first historical record
appeared some seven thousand years ago in what is now
known as Ireland. The Fairy Kingdom falls under the extensive phylum of Elementals that rank in the subtle order of
creation, whose cosmic substance becomes cryptic to finite
perception, and whose direct cause for genesis can be traced
as *divine workmen* for the natural world. Guided by higher
forces in the Universe (namely angels under the division of
Principalities, who govern the earth and all its inhabitants),
they come from the first order of the seven kingdoms of the
natural world. They reign supreme within the Elemental
Kingdom, which includes countless forms, including elves,
gnomes, nymphs, sprites, water spirits, devas, and dryads
to name just a few. They are considered "Spirits of Atoms"
because, while atomic, they still possess sentience and intelligence, although imperceptible to most human comprehension. Not unlike us, they, too, are subject to the universal laws
of karma.

The entire cosmos is controlled by an endless succession
of hierarchies maintained by sentient beings whose senses far
exceed our earthbound few. Science estimates that with all
five senses all we can perceive is one tenth of one percent of
all energies. So, in fact, we cannot assimilate or process 99.9
percent of the energies all around us. Is it any wonder we cannot see hierarchies beyond our own domain?

The scale of progressive involution down toward suba-
tomic beings presents a new series of never ending life cycles,
within an eternal field of potentiality that springs forth into
rates of vibration incomprehensible to our blind minds. In

other words, it's a polite way of saying that we're slower on the uptake than all the rest of creation.

The Fairy Kingdom is deeply integrated with our natural world as facilitators whose intelligence orchestrates the infinitesimal globules of life (or atoms) that compose all living things, such as rocks, flowers, plants, trees, rivers, ad infinitum. Their world intimately interfaces with ours, and therefore ours commands their immense concern, since we have decimated so much of their world while we systematically destroy our own. This explains their incarnation upon our plane of awareness, as they desperately attempt reconciliation between the natural world and the often-irrevocable desecration inflicted upon it.

Fairies tend to live near mountains, woods, and beaches, or any place where the natural world still maintains its omnipotent stretch. Due to their deep disgust of the Atlanteans and their successive reigns of destruction, the Fairies purposely waited for the Atlantean apex of incarnation to wane, before flitting in behind them to once again wage damage control upon their nemesis' insatiable lust for destruction.

They heal on a quantum level and thus can assess damage before it even occurs, viewing on a magnified scale the intensity of pollution and environmental decay. They maintain different hierarchies that oversee the principalities of nature, which includes life forms on land, mountains, forests, rivers, and seas, where the molecular structures are drastically changing and putting their fragile world at risk. They find news of oil tankard spillage utterly reprehensible, cannot stand to watch people chop down trees, and will go above and beyond duty to save a butterfly or not trample a flower, for these are their closest, dearest friends. It may sound strange to think of a flower as a friend, but you must remember anything that conducts a vibration of light has a consciousness. You may want to read *The Secret Life of Plants,* by Peter Tomkins and Christopher Bird, two scientists writing decades ago about how they could quantify scientifically that plants are sentient beings with feelings and emotion they could actually measure with a special meter.

If you ever have a member of this kingdom appear in your dreams, pay close attention, because they've usually got an important message for you from the natural world; it may be a warning or deep gratitude for respecting their delicate vibration. I once had one appear in an astral projection at a time when I couldn't make a decision because the more lucrative way would have impacted the plants and trees, while the other would have saved me great piles of money, time, and having to deal with other headaches. I went to bed that night and dreamt a fairy appeared in my childhood home, on the dishwasher. It was the brightest, neon, turquoise blue I have ever seen, it stood strong and silent and had a somber look on its face. It was so righteous and powerful, and stared so piercingly, it actually scared the living daylights out of me. It did not speak even when I spoke to it and seemed to just give a more incandescent glare. It was one of the few times in all my life I was terrified, and it got its message through to my conscious mind loud and clear. It also made me realize that as easily as I could cause trouble in its world, it could cause trouble in mine. I realized that later when it haunted me that it would land on a machine, in a house, not on a tree or bush outside. Yes, I made the more expensive decision because that fairy, though barely twelve inches tall, pretty much bullied me into submission without saying a word.

In Scotland there's a town called Findhorn, where plants, vegetation, and anything that sprouts does so on a monolithic scale. Many botanists, scientific groups, and universities have tried to crack the code of why things grow so large and lavishly there—even though the town was originally built on sand dunes. The town folk have a firm belief in deva and fairy energy and work with them intimately. They try to tell the researchers what's going on but they are met with condescending looks and sarcasm, as science plods along trying to figure out if there's some special soil or rain, or some other freak variable, that makes things there grow to monumental sizes. Science still cannot understand this blatant repudiation of their investigations, but people who live there are all in the know and just keep prospering with their mind-blowing blossoms.

Icelandic people take the elf and fairy realm to a whole new level, and call them Huldufolk, which means "hidden folk." The builders have to meet special criteria in order not to disturb the natural worlds where they are believed to frolic and dance. In 1982, one hundred-fifty Icelanders went to the NATO base in Keflavik to defend "Fairies and elves who might be endangered by American Phantom jets and AWACS reconnaissance planes." In 2011, elves/huldufólk were believed by some to be responsible for an incident in Bolungarvik where rocks pummeled residents in the streets, after a noted fairy residence had been disturbed. Icelandic gardens often feature tiny wooden álfhól (fairy houses) for them to live in. Some Icelanders have also built tiny churches to convert elves to Christianity (I suppose fairies could use a good dose of guilt when they're tempted to misuse those wands). Elves and fairies often appear in the dreams of Icelanders, and are usually described as wearing nineteenth-century Icelandic clothing in the color green. In the Faroe Islands they are supposedly black haired and wear grey. They dwell in mounds and detest churches, crosses, and electricity.

On rare occasions, they can emerge direct from their secret sphere, appearing in orbs of white light, magnified in size, sometimes seen dancing in circles near starlit woods. They mind boggle the unsuspecting observers, who forever treasure the day they once saw some divine creature they swore seemed, "no bigger than a thumb."

Invocation to Morgan le Fey and/or the fairy world:

"Fairy Queen Morgan, please help me protect and shelter the natural world we so desperately need. Would you please ask your squadron of fairies to help me with (name concern). I am forever grateful that you helped this member of your world and shall always respect your powers in the Fairy Kingdom."

If you have a crystal of any sort, it's good to hold or place on your third eye to make better contact with this particularly radiant being.

"There is always a solution. Some are in the shadows and some are bright like stars, but in the end all I want for you and your opponent is a win-win situation."

Thoughts from the mind of Forseti

CHAPTER 29

Forseti

A Norse god invoked for legal issues, mediation, arbitration, divorce, or anything where you must deal with justice and come to reconciliation. The ultimate peacemaker, Forseti spins miracles when one truly desires a fair outcome, and he's a compassionate being once invoked.

In a sumptuous palace called Glitnir, Forseti lives and holds spirit court where all legal disputes are turned into wins for all parties, before sifting down to the physical world. Glitner, according to ancient legend, has a roof of silver supported by red-gold pillars. These symbolic representations are portents of accessing the higher realm of spirit, since they include silver and gold, the highest frequencies of vibratory calibration, and the red represents earth-bound disputes.

Forseti facilitates overcoming the fear that comes with having to defend yourself—especially when your back's against the wall, and you need protection from cerebral attack and emotional exhaustion. His energy presents divine fate and inspires one to do the right thing even in the harshest circumstance. He can almost be thought of as a karmic arbitrator who ensures all scores are balanced and fair.

We live in a litigious society and one estimate suggests that the average American will be sued five times in one lifetime, when even once can knock your socks off and destroy your life. It's so easy to acquire things, but the unexpected mandate requires one maintain and protect them. Life simply isn't fair, and the energies are often stacked against you, but invoking a wise, benevolent being to preside over your legal affairs will push your potential for winning into the stratosphere.

I have seen many of my clients in a desperate bid to save home, children, jobs, and even pets, who've been accused of the wrong thing. When I explain to them the support they could engage, they tentatively invoke this spirit, but then achieve improbable results even in the most desperate situations. One scared mother fighting for full custody of her young son, said in court she had to make her defense. She invoked Forseti, and when she began to speak she felt a power come over her terrified voice and did not actually feel like she was the one speaking. She didn't stutter or trip over words, and her defense came out solid and strong to the point her ex-husband, stupefied by her strength, screamed out in the middle of the courtroom, "*That's ludicrous!*" My client won custody of her son after this buffoon tail-spun into a rage, where all could see his true colors.

There are countless stories, even in small interactions with ordinary people, you can invoke Forseti for, and rest assured his presence will provide the most optimal situation for winning.

Invocation to Forseti:

Wise Forseti, I ask you help me in this challenging situation (describe concern), where all I hope for is a balanced and fair outcome. I wish no harm to my fellow man, and thank you deeply for providing a win-win situation. Amen.

"I have come to be a protector unto thee. I waft unto thee air for thy nostrils, and the north wind which cometh forth from the god Tem unto thy nose. I have made whole for thee thy windpipe. I make thee to live like a god. Thine enemies have fallen under thy feet. I have made thy word to be true before Nut, and thou art mighty before the gods."

THE FUNERAL CHAMBER SPEECH OF ISIS,
The Egyptian Book of the Dead

CHAPTER 30

ISIS

n 4,500 BC, this **moon goddess** began her reign on the island of Philae in upper Egypt on the Nile delta, with worshippers spread throughout the Greco-Roman empire. The accepted dates for her reign are actually incorrect, since recently a hair comb was found by archeologists with the exact date inscribed upon it. It makes sense such a historical relic would be found, because the ancients believed the gods and goddesses controlled the weather when they combed their hair. She was worshipped as the ideal woman, matron of nature, magic, love, and sensuality, and can also be depicted as the protector of the dead and goddess of children. Her name means "throne" and on stone glyphs she's always seen with a throne upon her headdress.

According to the ancient legends, Isis married her brother Osiris (the standard practice to preserve royal dynastic bloodlines in that period), and loved him dearly. She often went away to help teach women how to become better housewives, but on arrival home from one such journey, found her beloved Osiris murdered in a jealous rage by his brother Set, the dark over-lord of chaos, storms, illness, rage, and confusion. He was said to be infertile, bisexual, with peculiar sexual predilections and regarded by all as a strange little man. Set even tried to rape Isis and Horus, and was thus regarded by ancients as a dangerous, violent god, though he had been kind many moons before his fall. Set had savagely retaliated against Osiris for having had a sexual encounter with his beloved wife Nepthys. Nepthys had pretended to be Isis and tricked Osiris into fornication, because her own husband Set was infertile and she wanted a baby. Set, upon discovery of this carnal liaison, chopped Osiris into fourteen pieces and threw them into the river.

Isis had enough on her silver platter, but coming home to find her husband dismembered merely galvanized her into reconstructing his mutilated body. She searched high and low for his bits and pieces, in order to put her beloved back together with her magical methods and secret incantations. She found every piece of his mutilated body except for one—his penis, which had been swallowed whole by a hungry carp. Isis was thus forced to make a magical penis, and that little nugget must have been erected with all the best bells and whistles since they soon bore a magnificent boy who would one day become the sun god, Horus.

Isis cults were found throughout every civilized society, including Africa; she inspired such devotion for many thousands of years because of her magical healing ability. Her legacy lives on as we discuss her most mystical instrument, the sistrum, a fork-shaped device that had small tambourine-like jingles that were meant to sound like the wind going through the papyrus plants, a sound that pleased the gods.

Isis and others gods and goddesses are often depicted with the sistrum (not to be confused with the ankh), a rattle used to move blocked energy that causes disease or any sort of malevolent vibration. Isis believed sound was the way in which to move stagnant energy that caused pain, discomfort, and disease. The rattle was then held close to the energy field around the body as one asked the gods to remove any malady or improve a situation. It was also implemented by the Native Americans and other indigenous tribes, and made with turtle shells, gourds, and buffalo scrotums. These tools are what inspired percussion instruments later on in modern life.

Any kind of rattle will do, even a baby rattle. Feel yourself relax as you close your eyes and shake the rattle all around your body, while asking Isis to help you heal a disorder. Be open to receive as you breathe in her healing propensities. Be sure to thank her as you breathe out.

Invocation to Isis:

Goddess of the Moon, I invoke your healing powers. Please help heal my (name situation) and allow the golden light of your power to fill my soul. I thank thee Isis for restoring this situation and only ask you accept my humble thanks. Amen.

If you wish to see the actual temple for Isis in Egypt, go to YouTube and search:

Visit to the Temple of Isis at Philae

"*No one is to be called an enemy; all are your benefactors, and no one does you harm. You have no enemy except yourselves.*"

St. Francis of Assisi (1181-1226)

CHAPTER 31

St. Francis of Assisi

Born in Umbria, Italy, living from 1181–1226, St. Francis of Assisi is a powerful saint you can invoke for any animal, under any circumstance. Our beloved saint, though not known for this other faculty, was also a gifted writer and scholars consider his works of astonishing grandeur. St. Francis is one of the most venerated religious figures in all recorded history; he's a power house and easy to access, and conducts miraculous intercessions. On his deathbed, St. Francis asked to see his donkey and thanked the gentle creature for carrying heavy loads and helping him throughout his life, and many watched as his donkey wept.

St. Francis was christened Giovanni di Bernardone (named after John the Baptist), but nicknamed by his father "Francesco," which means "Frenchman," because, unlike the other six children in the family, he picked up French from his mother and could even sing in it fluently. Francesco, as so often seen, was born into an extremely wealthy family. As he got older, he was always in trouble with the law from carousing, drinking, and basically acting like a juvenile delinquent. A part-time soldier (In Italy it's required by law that every boy perform military service for two years), his behavior got so out of control, he found himself in a Perugia jail for a whole year. It was here, in a filthy, stark, and lonely cell, he had a spiritual epiphany, where the crucifix leaped off the wall as he heard Jesus say, "Serve the master, not the man." Jesus also told him he was "leading a terrible life of sin." This impacted Francis so profoundly that upon his release, he immediately began helping the sick and the poor.

One famous story was when Francis was selling his father's wares in the market a beggar asked him for alms. Francis didn't know what to do and shook his head no. After the beggar walked away, Francis was so overcome with compassion, he ran after him and emptied his pockets out, giving the man every last cent he'd made that day. Francis' rich friends mocked him for being so soppy, but his father was livid that he'd given away what the father had worked so hard for him to earn.

Francis found it impossible to be around his privilege and wealth where no one seemed to care about the struggles of the people around them. In a desperate bid for enlightenment, he began living in a cave, where again he heard the crucifix loudly decree, "Francis, Francis, go and repair my house, which as you can see is falling into ruins." In response, needing funds to pay for the old church that was indeed collapsing; he sold his father's prized horse and the expensive cloth from his father's factory to pay for the supplies. When his father found out what Francis had done, he became enraged and wanted to punish his son for such blatant insolence. Hearing his father screaming his name outside of the church, Francis hid inside, praying to God his father wouldn't find him.

Several days later Francis finally emerged and was met by townsfolk who booed and pelted him with tomatoes, and, to his horror, his waiting father who shackled him to a tree and beat him as the townsfolk cheered. His father, not unlike everyone around, thought Francis was insane. He publicly disowned Francis, making him give up his vast inheritance in restitution for having the audacity to sell his beloved horse and expensive cloth. In the final degradation, his father ripped off his clothes and forced him to wear a laborer's cloth, painting a giant white cross upon it so all the world would see what a crazed fanatic his son really was.

Over time, Francis renounced his family before a magistrate, and started preaching on the streets, still wearing the laborer's robe with the cross—to his proud family's utter mortification—and he actually attracted twelve followers. His disciples replicated the same robe, but for an even more dramatic effect shaved off the hair at the top of their heads, as they went around preaching the word. Francis completed the first replica of a three-dimensional holy manger using a live ox and donkey for a realistic effect at the local church. That night when he went to sleep, he had a divine vision of an angel speaking intensely to him. Brother Leo, who was near St. Francis at the time, documented the precise account told to him by St. Francis: "Suddenly he saw a vision of a seraph, a six-winged angel on a cross. This angel gave him the gift of the five wounds of Christ."

Upon awakening, Francis found blood pouring out of gaping stigmata in his hands and feet, where there were not only holes, but big black marks from the nails that were bent where Jesus was nailed to the cross. In addition to these painful bleeding ulcers, a giant sword slash emerged on his side and this one oozed pus. Over time, Francis became ashamed of these marks and tried to hide them under his robe.

Pope Innocent III caught wind of the humble preacher and, thanks to a dream and a supportive bishop, reluctantly endorsed his order in 1210. Francis then founded the Order of The Poor Clares, because of a girl named Clare from Assisi who wanted to join him, as did her brother and many other local boys and girls. Fran's own order grew not just through Italy but France, Germany, Hungary, Spain, and the Far East, taking on an inordinate amount of supporters, though they were clad in rough garments, had taken vows of poverty, and had to live their life in bare feet.

The disciples themselves performed miracles, one in particular after his death: Brother Peter Catani, who was buried in Porziuncola, where Francis and many of the disciples lived. Numerous miracles were attributed to his graveside and people started flocking to it, disturbing the strict life of the Franciscans. St. Francis became so aggravated by the swarming people, he prayed and demanded Brother Pete to "stop performing" all miracles immediately and obey his commands in death as he had done in life. The miracles immediately, to the disenchantment of a seeking public, stopped.

St. Francis suffered tremendous pain from his stigmata and from a debilitating eye disease, and went to several cities in the hopes he could be healed. In the end, he went back to his hut in Poeziuncola, where it all began. He knew the end was near, and spent the last days of his life surrounded by scribes who took down dictation on his spiritual insights. He died on the eve of October 3, 1226, while singing psalms.

I could write multiple books on St. Francis alone, and you may want to access some of his highly regarded works, and there's a reason I saved him for last. This Saint's love for animals was profound. He spent so much time in isolation praying, his sensitivity to and respect for the creatures became supremely heightened. It was witnessed time after time that he had a distinct connection to them, and one story in particular can be testified by a multitude of witnesses.

In the city of Gubbio, where Francis lived for several years, a gigantic wolf (they can get up to 175 pounds and stretch seven feet long) started eating livestock, pets, and the occasional human being. Francis went up the hill to find the wolf and give him a good tongue lashing, and although fear of the wolf caused his many supporters to flee as they ascended up the mountain, the saint kept climbing with just a few stragglers accompanying him. Finding the wolf in all its glory ready to pounce on this newest home delivered meal, St. Francis made the sign of the cross and commanded the wolf to sit down. The wolf closed his jaws, walked over and lay down at Francis's feet as he spoke to the wolf. "Brother Wolf, you do much harm in these parts and you have done great evil," said Francis. "All these people accuse you and curse you...But brother wolf, I would like to make peace between you and the people." Francis then effortlessly led the wolf down the hill and into the village to the gasps of the townsfolk watching. Surrounded by startled citizens, he made a pact between them and the wolf. The wolf had "done evil out of starvation," so St. Francis said the townsfolk were now to "feed the wolf every day. In return the wolf will no longer eat you." St. Francis also made a pact with the town dogs, which were forbidden from barking at the wolf since it made him distressed. Francis then blessed the wolf and the townsfolk fed him and that was the end of the attacks.

This indicates that some animals are much more than we suspect—as are many humans. The force that intermingles with our mind and personality can be divine or downright infernal. In general, much of the animal world is good, and has been put here to do reconnaissance for God, to test our true levels of loving capacity and see if we can go beyond our self-indulgence to extend love to the most vulnerable of all living things. In the Bible it says, "Be not forgetful to entertain strangers: for thereby some have entertained angels unaware." (Hebrews 13:2) Whoever said the "strangers" were human?

There is also another quote to back up this belief. "Take heed that ye despise not one of these little ones; for I say unto you, that in heaven their angels always behold the face of my Father which is in heaven." (Mathew 18:10) Whoever said the "little ones" were children? Of course we know *they* have angels, but Mathew underscored the "little ones," and due to translation issues, "little ones" could have easily been misinterpreted from "inferior ones," meaning animals. So be wary, because some animals may be angels, not to mention have their own guardian angel, and learn to love anything that has eyes to see the sun—for they bring a portion of heaven hidden within them.

Native Americans believed animals stood on a bridge that linked us to the divine, and decided who could come or go through the gates of heaven:

When a human dies there is a bridge they must cross to enter into Heaven. At the head of the bridge waits every animal that human encountered during their lifetime. The animals, based on what they know of this person, decide which humans may cross the bridge…and which are turned away.
Navajo Prayer

The ancient Egyptians emphatically felt animals were divine, and when you put the pieces together, it all makes sense. Be warned, reader, for their eyes are like periscopes stretching out from the furthest ports of heaven.

Invocation to Saint Francis:

Saint Francis, please assist me in (finding, saving, helping, etc.) the creature(s) I hold dear. I ask for your help because of your deep love for the animal kingdom. Thank you, St. Francis, for your wise and powerful intercession. I know you will help the soul of the creature(s) I love, and am so deeply grateful. Make me a channel of your peace. Amen.

There are so many videos of St. Francis on YouTube, I thought it would be good to show you four in particular. First is a video I made to help you talk with animals, the second shows where Francis spent most of his life, the third is a beautiful, short reenactment of his life, and the fourth is a glimpse into the secret world of the blessing of his tomb by the Franciscan order of priests he incepted. Be sure to breathe in the energy of these videos; there have been miracles triggered just by gazing at his tomb.

Go to YouTube and search for:

Communicate with Any Animal
or
Assisi Tour
or
St Francis of Assisi—Mickey Rourke—Porziuncola
or
At the tomb of St. Francis

CHAPTER 32

Closing Thoughts

Life in the Spider's Web

"Spiders are patient and meticulous," reminds Kuan Yin. "Humans sometimes believe insects are insignificant because they are small. However, their work is of great importance to the world. Be still and watch the spider build its web."

There may be some of you reading this book who think I've exaggerated to get a few points across. Nothing could be further from the truth. If anything, I've left big globs of information out—not on purpose, but due to erased or faded memories. These beings are real, and many appeared who I couldn't have possibly conjured up since I didn't even know they existed before we "met." Somewhere in our DNA these old harmonics thrive, and all we have to do to is quiet our minds and listen. Science estimates that 95 percent of our DNA is "junk"—perhaps that's where we hide our past lives and where critical directives secretly stream to and from our soul. The more you get used to communicating with the spirits, the more they reply. I'm sure that's precisely why age-old civilizations built lavish temples for thousands of years and had their deities emblazoned on their coins, because the ancients knew the critical component of respect. They were far more brilliant in certain arenas than we are today, and where they reigned supreme was the secret kingdom of the soul. They knew how to access the transpersonal dimensions, and considered prayers useless without it. We are now coming to a precipice, where we will either reconnect to our hidden self in a more potent way, or leave what was once authentic reality far, far behind.

We all know what virtual reality is and use it constantly, as we insert ourselves into the world of the computer. By the year 2030, however, the computer will inject itself into ours—and we won't have the option to block it. Like insects trapped in a spider's web, we will lose our autonomy and become part of a snare impossible to escape. Energy even from where we once were will be able to be tracked, as we enter into the formidable realm of *augmented reality*. Computers will be interfaced so deeply into daily life, we won't know where we end and they begin. We will actually have the Internet in our contact lenses (they already have the prototype), avatar secretaries in our walls, and the intelligence of the ages in a cheap, hand-held device. It all sounds grand, but what we should brace ourselves for is a massive collapse of the self. To fall in love, get married, go on vacation—all done in these magical fantasy worlds, doing it as that person we secretly longed to be, and all at the press of a button—will seduce even the humblest, making augmented reality the bright, shiny new addiction.

Actuality will be some dark, dim place we barely know and as that dissolves, so, too, does our sense of self and our belief in our own purpose. We will be strangers in a strange land if we allow brainwashing by a distorted reality we'll soon be force-fed to believe. It could be a staggering experience if we only hold tight to our true selves, engaging with this brand new world as an addendum to our own, buckled-down reality.

Future theorists believe that as we move forth into this bold new age, computer chips will become so disposable they'll be slotted into every rock, tree, and flower including every hole, nook, and cranny that can be perceived. They believe this will give rise to the mysticism of the Middle Ages, since inanimate objects will now have a voice. Maybe the quote of the Blue Fairy speaking to a wooden Pinocchio wasn't so far off the mark when she said,

> "Little puppet made of pine, awake.
> The gift of life is thine."

Perhaps this intimacy will open our fragile minds to a world we cannot leave behind. This magical perspective from our computer-generated society may, in fact, connect us closer to spirit, and in the end bring us back to that most elusive place, ourselves.

With well over fifteen thousand case studies, the author's established psychic practice in London remains popular throughout all of Europe. Her clients have ranged from inspectors at Scotland Yard to top models in Paris. Integrating modern psychology with ancient metaphysics, the author has developed breakthrough methodologies that thoroughly activate psychic sensing. Thought impossible to attain, these techniques have never before been analyzed and diagramed, though tested and perfected through the multitude of students the author has trained.

Attending the London College of Psychic Studies in England for nearly fifteen years, and granted access to the inner circles for advanced psychic development, the author apprenticed with the most distinguished psychics, mediums, and healers of our time. Many of her teachers were people born during the Victorian era, who now help her constantly from the spirit world.

At the institution formerly known as the Royal College for Medical Hypnosis and Psychotherapy at the NHS Hospital in Blackheathe, England, the author trained in hypnoanaesthesia for surgery and applied psychology with the world-renowned Dr. John Butler PhD (London) MBSH, CHT, MA, BA (Hons.), DHP. The school, now known as the Hypnotherapy Training Institute of Britain, was where she learned classical clinical hypnosis and applied psychology and psychotherapy. Doctor Butler has been known as the leading and foremost distinguished teacher of hypnotherapy in the world, teaching accredited courses from Kings College and The Royal College of Anesthetics in London, England. The author uses these world class techniques with her metaphysical students at her school and live online classes, in order to induct them into an altered state. Here consciousness can be launched, in order to reach levels of relaxation impossible to achieve on one's own. In this altered state, one can reach the remote portions of the brain and access something that can only be described as soul.

Angel also refined psycho-spiritual studies with the National Federation of Spiritual Healers in England, who work in libraries, hospitals, and other public facilities. Her formal education also includes two years of understudies in psychology at Ohio University, before graduating from the prestigious DSL postgraduate in West London, known for its hard-core curriculum in ancient and classical studies.

Nominated as a runner-up in the 2004 *Writer's Digest Competition* for *New Voices in Literature Award*, the author now lives in Aspen, Colorado. A psychic-medium Angel does consultations with people from all around the world, in person or face-to-face on the computer. The author also teaches classical metaphysics at her established psychic school, The Academy of Light, as well as live classes online, with principles based on ancient mystery school studies. Her waiting list includes high-profile celebrities, producers, politicians, doctors, lawyers, professors, Hollywood screenwriters, super-models, philanthropists, scientists, investors, Grammy winners, and psychoanalysts. She has also written a dozen short articles on psychedelic thought in the formerly known magazine *The Healix*, and has a website at,

www.angelcusick.com

YouTube is an ongoing resource where many of her principles of thought are elucidated and video-streamed to an ever-growing public, which can be found by going to www.YouTube.com and search for,

http://www.youtube.com/user/AngelBlog

Made in the USA
Lexington, KY
09 September 2012